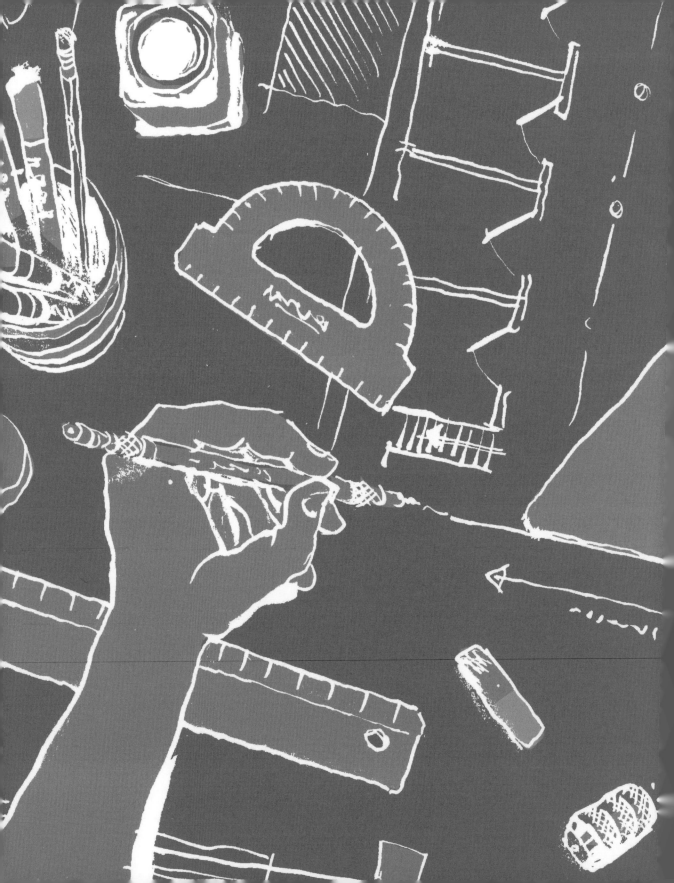

The Little Book of
Architectural History
for Children and
Curious Grown-Ups

The Li
of Arc
Histor

Mogens Andreassen Morgen
with illustrations by Claus Nørregaard

ttle Book
hitectural
y

for Children and
Curious Grown-Ups

Strandberg Publishing

Contents

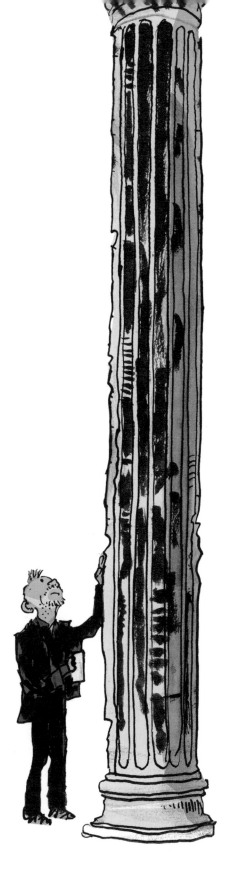

*For Albert, Linnea, Salina, Pernille
– and other curious souls*

A short introduction

As you read this introduction, you are probably in a work of architecture, because architecture is all around us. And even if you have never given it much thought, architecture has a big impact on how you see and experience the world.

More than 2,000 years ago, the Roman architect and engineer Vitruvius wrote that architecture should possess *strength*, *function* and *beauty*. This makes architecture different from other arts: it should meet certain practical purposes and be built to last – ideally, for a long time. It is remarkable that Vitruvius's definition of architecture is still the most precise definition that exists.

Knowing architectural history is useful, because it is like a large library full of inspiration. For example, the Colosseum in Rome (see page 26), which was built almost 2,000 years ago, can be a great source of inspiration for architects designing a new football stadium today. And Startup Lions Campus on the banks of Lake Turkana in Kenya (see page 160), which was completed in 2021, can inspire architects who want to create sustainable architecture that uses local materials and is adapted to the local climate.

But the history of architecture is long and complex, and it would be impossible to describe all the buildings in the world.

So how do you get a grasp of this huge field? One way is to divide history into periods. That often works well in scientific contexts, but the sharp distinctions risk oversimplifying the topic, since the periods have always overlapped and influenced each other.

The Little Book of Architectural History for Children and Curious Grown-Ups gives you an introduction through 50 selected works of architecture. The oldest of them is more than 4,500 years old. I selected these because they have all played an important role in architectural history – and because I think they are fabulous and make me dream about the wonders of architecture. As you read the 50 stories, you might have your own ideas about how they connect. You might even discover connections that architectural historians have never thought of!

I have visited most of the buildings in the book, and pretty soon, I hope to visit the rest. It is important to go inside the buildings and experience them with all your senses. Hopefully, the book will also inspire you to get out there. You can always hop on your bike – although, if you plan to see all the buildings, it is going to be a long bike ride!

Mogens Andreassen Morgen

Prehistory and antiquity

Until around 1000

Our ability to build has played an important role in making us who we are. Inside our houses, huts and tents, we could shelter from the environment and find peace and quiet to improve our skills.

Living together in small communities allowed us to share the labour and get even better at our individual jobs. We learned to grow food and keep animals, so that we did not have to rely only on hunting or gathering fruits and berries. We also developed crafts, not least in order to improve our homes.

Through farming and trade, small towns grew richer and developed into major civilizations. At this stage, we began to build impressive monuments to honour local gods and rulers. Many of these monuments are still around today.

The word 'architecture' comes from one of these civilizations: in ancient Greek, 'arkhitekton' meant master builder. Over time, the meaning of the word has become much more complex, and today, architects not only build houses but also work with life in between the houses.

The Primitive Hut and the birth of architecture

What is architecture? And what elements does it consists of? Those were some of the questions that the French priest Marc-Antoine Laugier asked himself when he wrote his *Essay on Architecture* in 1753. The book contains a drawing that is now even better known than the text. The drawing shows a 'primitive hut' consisting of four trees that support a simple roof made of branches and leaves. In the foreground, a woman is sitting on some fragments of classical architecture as she points out the cabin to an angel standing next to her.

The drawing shows us the birth of architecture. The hut is a house in its most basic form: columns, beams and a roof. The drawing shows that architecture is essentially about creating a shelter, and that good architecture is based on principles we can find in nature. Laugier argued that architecture, which the woman in the picture is turning her back to, had become much too refined and 'artificial'. Instead, people should return to the primitive hut, a simpler and more logical form of architecture designed to meet basic human needs. Laugier thought that anything else was just superfluous decoration.

Laugier's call for simple and 'honest' architecture has been repeated many times throughout history. His essay has taken on renewed importance today, as we are beginning to understand the close connection between humans and nature. This connection also calls on us to develop a simpler architecture that is in harmony with planet Earth.

Great Pyramid of Giza, Egypt. Completed around 2560 BC under Pharaoh Khufu.

The mysterious pyramid

Only one of the seven wonders of the ancient world is still standing today: the Great Pyramid of Giza in Egypt. This impressive monument was built about 4,600 years ago and remains a mystery to this day. Why does the pyramid look the way it does, and how were the ancient Egyptians able to build such a giant structure?

The Great Pyramid stands on the edge of the Sahara, outside the city of Cairo.

With its simple, geometric design – rising from a square footprint, with sides that measure 230 metres each and four triangular faces that come together in a soaring tip about 140 metres above the desert sand – the pyramid looks majestic. When it was new, it was covered with smooth white stones. Its corner edges were so sharp they must have looked as if you could cut yourself on them.

The pyramid was built as a tomb for Pharaoh Khufu. To get inside, you go through a hidden entrance and several long corridors that slope both up and down inside the vast mass of stone. The burial chamber is placed in the centre of the pyramid. Here, Khufu's mummy lay in a stone sarcophagus, surrounded by treasures to make sure he had a good afterlife.

Since the ancient Egyptian kingdom crumbled, there have been many wild theories about the pyramid. Some people speculated that the Egyptian builders might have used 'number magic' to calculate the building's geometric shape and that it might have held mystical meaning. The Serbian physicist Nikola Tesla, whom the electric cars are named after, was deeply fascinated by the pyramid. He spent a long time studying it to see if it might have been designed to transmit electrical signals, like a giant antenna. And if you're a fan of science fiction, there are even theories that aliens from outer space helped the Egyptians build the enormous monument!

The pyramid is believed to have been built over a period of 20 to 30 years by thousands of workers who cut the stone blocks from a nearby quarry and dragged them into place, one by one.

The Great Pyramid of Giza is the largest pyramid in Egypt, but it is far from the only one. If you sail down the Nile, you will see that it is part of a large burial site, where several generations of Egyptian pharaohs lie buried. To date, more than 80 pyramids have been discovered. These show how the Egyptians gradually improved their skills as architects and builders. There are also pyramids both in Central and South America, even though there has been no contact between the people there and the Egyptians.

The Great Pyramid of Giza marks the beginning of architecture and the establishment of fundamental principles related to geometry, materials, weight and humans' relationship with the cosmos. The pyramid also shows that these early builders were extremely skilled and that architects were able to calculate volumes and angles with a degree of mathematical precision that is impressive even today.

Divine proportions

In the middle of the Greek capital, Athens, the hill of Acropolis towers over the city. At the top of the hill lies the Parthenon. This beautiful temple was built more than 2,400 years ago. It was dedicated to the goddess Athena whom the city is also named after.

The Parthenon was designed by the architects Iktinos and Kalikrates and took 10 years to build. The temple had 46 outer columns in Doric style with a horizontal beam on top called an architrave. At either end of the temple, there are two triangular gables decorated with sculptures. In the space between the architrave and the gable, there is a frieze with a three-dimensional picture carved in stone. The frieze shows scenes from Greek mythology, including centaurs, giants and amazons.

The decorations are the work of the sculptor Phidias, who also created a 10-metre-tall statue of Athena in gold and ivory for the innermost hall inside the temple.

Many of the statues are now gone, and the ones that remain are all white. However, that is not how they looked during antiquity. Back then they were painted in an explosion of colours, which has since worn off.

The structure forms a large rectangle, measuring about 69 x 31 metres. If you calculate the ratio between the two lengths, you'll see that the longer side is about 2.25 times longer than the shorter side. This ratio is repeated in many parts of the building, for example in the gable, which is 2.25 times wider than it is tall, and in the distance between the columns, which is 2.25 times the width of the columns. This ratio of 1:2.25 – or 4:9, as it is often written – is an example of the ancient Greek concept of 'divine proportions'. If architects made sure to repeat these proportions throughout the building, it would become more beautiful and harmonious. Therefore, this particular ratio must have divine qualities, they concluded.

If we take a closer look, we will find that the building is not as straight as it seems. The architects knew that too many straight lines could make it look rigid. That is why the columns are not completely vertical but lean about 7 centimetres towards the centre of the structure. Each column is shaped with so-called entasis, meaning that it bulges slightly in the middle. The platform that the temple is built on is about 12 centimetres taller in the middle, which makes the whole thing look as if it curves upwards. It is an optical illusion, because all the curves are so subtle that you do not notice them consciously. But without them, the temple would not have been as beautiful as it is.

If you visit Athens today, you will only find the ruins of the original Parthenon temple. The building was badly damaged in a wartime bombardment in 1687, because it was used to store gunpowder. Still, the Parthenon remains one of the most important works of architecture from Greek antiquity – a period that has had tremendous influence on European architecture. In our journey through architectural history, the inspiration from Greek temples will show up again and again. Architects will always have a relationship with antiquity.

Carved into the rock

You arrive to the ancient Arabian city of Petra after a 1.5-kilometre walk through a long, narrow gorge that cuts through a tall mass of red sandstone. In some places, the gorge is just a few metres wide, while the red rock towers 100 metres above. The contrast is striking when you step out of the narrow passage and onto the large square of Petra, where giant temple facades are carved into the rockface. Here, people lived in rooms carved into the rock, just like the earliest humans, who sought shelter from the elements in natural caves.

Petra had been inhabited since prehistoric times, but the architecture we see the ruins of today was created about 2,200 years ago. Petra was the main city of the Nabataeans, an ancient Arabian people. Here, they had control of the stream of merchants who took their caravans through the gorge on their way from the Mediterranean Sea in the west to Mesopotamia in the east, or from southern Arabia to Damascus in the north. The Nabataeans were masters of water regulation and made Petra a desert oasis in this dry Jordanian landscape.

The many temples and the remains of a large theatre show that Petra was densely populated. At its height, the city had almost 40,000 inhabitants. The most famous temple is the Treasury, al-Khazneh, with its impressive 40-metre-tall facade full of columns and statues. Behind the facade lies a closed burial chamber, which is believed to have once held a stone sarcophagus.

Petra speaks to the imagination, and it is not surprising that Tintin visited the city in the comic book *The Red Sea Sharks*. Or that the American film director Steven Spielberg used the al-Khazneh Treasury as a set for his film *Indiana Jones and the Last Crusade*.

The fascination with the city stems not just from the fact that it was cut directly into the rock but also from the beautiful detailing. The amazing facades make a big impression in the context of the inhospitable natural scenery. Petra is a stunning place on earth, where nature and culture blend into one.

A Roman space

The Italian capital, Rome, is home to some of the oldest structures in the history of architecture. Rome is also where we find the oldest building in the world that is still in use: the temple of Pantheon, which was built nearly 2,000 years ago under the Roman Emperor Hadrian.

In ancient Greek, 'pan' means 'all', and 'theo' means 'god'. In other words, the Pantheon was not dedicated to one specific Roman god but to all of them, from Jupiter, the god of thunder, and Mars, the god of war, to Venus, the goddess of love.

The Pantheon has a monumental appearance and a commanding presence in the narrow Roman streets. The porch, which faces the Rotonda square, consists of an open, covered room with 16 large columns, each carved from a single huge piece of rock.

From the porch, you continue into a vestibule, where two large bronze doors lead into the main space. Here, you are struck by the building's overwhelming beauty and size. The walls form a 43-metre-wide cylinder that is

21.5 metres tall. On top of this cylinder, a circular dome adds another 21.5 metres to the height of the building. This means that there are 43 metres from the floor to the top of the dome – exactly the same measurement as the width of the cylinder.

The underside of the dome has five layers of coffers: four-sided sunken panels that gradually get smaller towards the middle of the dome. This gradual change in size causes an optical illusion that makes the top of the dome seem even farther away. At the very top you will find the Pantheon's oculus, or 'eye': a round opening with a diameter of 8.2 metres.

This eye is the building's only source of light and creates a magical effect, as if the opening were the sun itself, lighting up the earth from outer space. On rainy days, rain falls inside the building and creates a unique atmosphere of sound. At mid-day in spring and autumn equinox, the light of the sun falling through the eye strikes the large portal leading into the vestibule. This is believed to be a deliberate design feature intended to make the Pantheon appear like an image of the universe itself.

Over time, the Pantheon has been stripped of valuable building materials on several occasions. Among the things that were taken are a gold-plated bronze roof, marble wall cladding and bronze beams from the vestibule. Nevertheless, the interior structure is generally intact. This is both because the Pantheon was made of durable materials, such as brick and an early version of concrete, and because, over the years, it was put to new uses instead of being demolished.

Pantheon is a great example of the marvels of Roman engineering, so it's no surprise that the history of architecture is full of buildings that were inspired by its grand design.

Colosseum in Rome, Italy.
Built in 72–80 under Emperor
Vespasian (9–79) and his son
Emperor Titus (39–81).

Gladiator fights at the colossal Colosseum

The Colosseum is a gigantic amphi-theatre in Rome with room for 50,000 spectators. However, it was not named for its size but after a colossal statue of Emperor Nero that stood next to the amphitheatre.

The basic floor plan of the Colosseum is shaped like an ellipse measuring 188 x 156 metres. The outer wall is nearly 50 metres tall and clad with marble. The facade originally had 80 Roman arches divided into four stories that ran the full circumference of the build-ing: Doric columns at the bottom, Ionic columns above and Corinthian col-umns on top of those. The fourth level was a sort of attic – a top floor with a closed facade. Instead of colums, this level had pilasters – a half-column that appears to stick out of the wall.

This practice of dividing the facade into different orders of columns is also seen in later architecture, for example during the Renaissance.

The official opening of the building was marked with 100 days of celebrations. Here, spectators could witness gladi-ator fights, sometimes with wild ani-mals, as wells as dance performances and public executions. On some occa-sions, the arena was even filled with huge amounts of water and used to stage sea battles.

Today, the Colosseum appears as the essence of a beautiful, romantic ruin. But while most ruins are the result of slow decay, natural disasters, fires or other, similar events, the Colosseum was actually 'ruined' by Rome's own inhabitants. The building was used as a source of materials for new buildings in Rome. Fortunately, there is still enough of the Colosseum remaining for us to imagine the many big events that took place here.

Even now, almost 2,000 years later, the Colosseum continues to serve as a source of inspiration for the design of new stadiums. It is still difficult to find a more efficient way to fill and empty a stadium than through the Colosseum's numerous Roman arches. So, next time you enjoy a football match or a stadium concert, send a thought to the gladiator fights at the Colosseum!

Why do churches look the way they do?

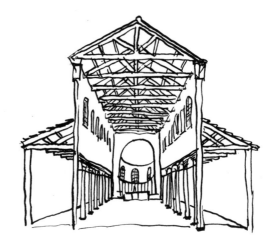

Ancient Rome was built on seven hills. The Basilica of Santa Sabina is an old church located on the Aventine Hill. It consists of a long room, called a nave, with spaces on either side, the so-called aisles. Nave and aisles are separated by rows of columns. The nave is wider and taller, which makes it possible to install windows in the facade above the columns to let in daylight. The entrance is placed at one end of the nave, with the altar located at the other end, in a semicircular room called an apse.

If you think this layout sounds familiar, you are not wrong. The basilica design has been used as a model for many churches around the world. But in fact, the basilica first appeared in Roman antiquity and had very different purposes, including public assembly halls, bathhouses and market halls. When Emperor Constantine the Great made Christianity legal in 313, the Romans also began using basilicas for worshipping the Christian god, and

this marked the beginning of a very long tradition.

Over the ages, the basilicas evolved as people began constructing vaulted ceilings in brick and adding spires. Some churches were designed with a transept, which made the layout look like a cross, and later, large windows were added in the tall nave, letting in lots of (heavenly) light.

The basilica is an example of a so-called typology: a category of buildings with similar forms and functions. As illustrated by Santa Sabina, some typologies date all the way back to classical antiquity. This means that the many churches all over the world can trace a direct line back to Rome's Aventine Hill.

A floating dome

When you arrive in Istanbul by train, it is fascinating to see how Hagia Sophia stands out and dominates the city's skyline with its dome and minarets. It was originally built as a Christian cathedral by the Byzantine emperor Justinian I. Despite its enormous size, it did not take long to complete. According to contemporary historical sources, about 10,000 workers were involved in building Hagia Sophia, and when it was finished, it was by far the largest church in Christendom.

The church was built mainly in brick with lavish decorations in marble and other precious types of stone. The huge dome has a diameter of about 31 metres and is almost 56 metres tall, and even today, it remains a mystery how the builders were able to construct such a large dome. Part of the explanation is the two large half-domes on either side and the smaller half-domes below, which support the structure.

Hagia Sophia has had different functions over the centuries. In 1453, when the Ottoman Empire conquered Istanbul – then called Constantinople – the church was converted into a mosque, and four minarets were added to the structure. A number of Christian images were also removed or covered up. In 1935, the mosque was turned into a museum, and the builders uncovered images that had been hidden for centuries. They also found some runes carved into the wall spelling out the names 'Halfdan' and 'Are'. They are believed to have been Vikings who had travelled all the way to Constantinople sometime in the 800s, working as body guards to the Byzantine emperor.

In 2020, the building was converted back to a mosque. The fact that it has been such a significant religious space for both Christians and Muslims reflects its enormous spiritual impact. Its divine atmosphere is underscored by the light pouring in through the many windows placed just under the dome. On a sunny day, the effect is magical and makes the dome appear to float.

Middle Ages

Around 1000 to 1400

When we talk about the Middle Ages, we often focus on dark times and misery. History books tell stories about the huge plague epidemic in Europe that killed at least 25 million people – about 40% of the population at the time. It was also a time of war and religious conflict, which made life insecure, and several years of bad weather led to harvest failure and widespread famine.

But there are also many positive stories to tell. Despite the colossal challenges, Europe's many small urban communities, abbeys and monasteries were bustling centres of new ideas and great art and architecture.

Strolling through the Middle Ages

If you want an idea of what life was like in the Middle Ages, you should visit Quedlinburg in Germany. The town, which is located in the mountainous region called the Harz, has more than 1,200 half-timbered houses, which was the most common type of house during the Middle Ages. The town is also home to Germany's oldest half-timbered building, dating all the way back to the 1400s.

Quedlinburg developed around a royal castle in the 900s. With its winding streets and town squares, it is one of the largest protected heritage sites in Germany. The medieval town plan and most of the buildings have been preserved, so we can see how the tradition of half-timbered construction has developed over the past many centuries.

A half-timbered house consists of a timber frame with a skeleton of vertical posts and horizontal links called interties. The space in between the timbers is filled out with various materials, including bricks or wattle and daub – a woven lattice of branches (wattle) covered (daubed) with clay. Because the structure is divided into many small sections, it is easy to expand the house or add doors or windows. You can even take the whole building apart and rebuild it somewhere else. In some half-timbered houses, the first floor sticks out slightly. This makes it possible to get a little more floor space without pushing too far into the street. Here, the transition between the two facades is often richly decorated with wooden carvings.

In a way, Quedlinburg can feel like a living museum, but it is also an active, modern town. It is worth considering why the narrow, crooked streets feel so pleasant to walk. Maybe it is because the scale of the buildings matches the size of the human body. Or maybe it has something to do with the use of high-quality materials and the town's mix of planned and unplanned buildings.

A visit to Quedlinburg is a very authentic experience. Today, young people come here to learn and practise traditional crafts through working on the old buildings. Passing these traditions on is an important condition for preserving our building culture for the future. Traditional building methods contain a lot wisdom that needs to be rediscovered in future architecture.

Without
a single nail

Urnes Stave Church is an exceptional
church. Constructed entirely of wood
without a single iron nail, it looks as
if it could have been built by Vikings
– and for good reason, since it was created around 1130, when builders still
knew and mastered Viking Age craft
traditions. The Vikings built ships that
could sail all the way to Greenland and
North America, and the Urnes Stave
Church demonstrates their amazing
woodwork traditions.

If you sail through the large Norwegian
Sognefjord, you will see the church,
perched beautifully on a mountain-
side overlooking the fjord. The church
was constructed around 16 posts, or
'staves', as they are called in Norwegian, which is what gave this building
method its name. The wooden architecture copies Romanesque stone
architecture in many ways. For example, it has columns with capitals and
arches as part of the construction. It
also has a plank ceiling, and the roof is
covered with beautifully finished
wooden shingles and topped by a ridge
turret, a small tower.

Stave churches represent some of the most advanced medieval building methods, which is why they have survived for 1,000 years. One of the secrets is that the timber structure is able to move with the wind in the harsh Norwegian climate, because the joints have no nails or screws. If the structure was not able yield slightly, the church might well have collapsed centuries ago. This same flexibility is also what enabled Viking ships to survive violent storms at sea.

Urnes Stave Church has a classical basilica floor plan with aisles, a chancel and an apse. It has two entrances: the main entrance to the west and a large portal on the north side. The decorations on the north-facing portal are world-famous because they are the only preserved example of a particular three-dimensional style. The pattern resembles snakes intertwined in a fight to the death, possibly symbolizing the Christian idea of the battle between good and evil. The tall nave also features beautiful decorations, with posts adorned by Biblical images and carvings of plants and mythical creatures. These decorations are an important link between pre-Christian Nordic culture and medieval Christianity. Furthermore, the similarity of these ornaments to Celtic art suggests a connection to Britain and Ireland.

Urnes Stave Church is the oldest stave church in the world and stands as one of the most sophisticated medieval wooden constructions in this part of the world. Today, as architects are beginning to look into the sustainability of wooden architecture, we can learn a lot from the outstanding quality of the woodwork of Urnes Stave Church.

A forest of columns

From outside, the Mezquita in Córdoba looks like a fortress with its tall sandstone walls topped by parapets. When you step inside the building, it is like opening a treasure chest. You find yourself in a forest of columns that support colourful double arches in red brick and yellowish sandstone. The room has a magical atmosphere, as if it had come straight out of the story collection *One Thousand and One Nights*.

The Moors were a Muslim people who conquered much of Spain and Portugal around 711. They made the city of Córdoba their capital and began to build the large Mezquita, which is the Spanish word for 'mosque'. The city grew, and by the 900s, more than half a million people lived there. Therefore, the Mezquita was expanded several times until it reached the enormous size it has today.

You enter the building through the Patio de los Naranjos, meaning the Courtyard of Orange Trees. Originally, this was a garden with wells, where worshippers could draw water for the ritual Muslim washing before entering the mosque. On the side towards the courtyard, the 54-metre-tall bell tower stands high above the roofs of the other buildings in Córdoba.

The tower has undergone many changes over the years, but it has always served the same basic purpose. The original Muslim minaret was used to call the faithful to prayer, just as the bell calls Christian worshippers to service.

The Mezquita is a beautiful mix of Islamic and Christian architecture. Archaeological excavations show that there was a Christian basilica on the site before the mosque was built, and when the Catholics conquered Córdoba in 1236, they did not destroy the mosque but instead transformed it into a Christian cathedral. In the 1500s, a large new cathedral was built inside the mosque but without destroying the original architecture.

One of the clear traces of the Moors is the stunningly beautiful patterns and mosaics on walls and ceilings. Since Islam forbids images of God, the building is instead decorated with calligraphy and geometric floral decorations. But the most impressive feature is the seemingly endless rows of interior arcades. It is a truly magical architectural universe that is revealed when you enter the Mezquita.

*Notre-Dame in Paris, France.
Built around 1163–1345 by
the Catholic church.*

The hunchback of Notre-Dame

Most people know about the hunchback of Notre-Dame – at least from the Disney animation film. The book that inspired the film tells the story of the humpbacked bell-ringer Quasimodo and his love for the beautiful Esmeralda, but in a way, the Notre-Dame cathedral itself is the true lead character thanks to the vivid and lyrical descriptions of the building.

Notre-Dame is located on the small island Île de la Cité in the Seine river in the middle of Paris. Construction began in 1163 and took almost 100 years to complete. The church is about 40 metres wide and 130 metres long. From the entrance, the nave leads up to the altar at the opposite end. In the middle, there is a transept, which gives the design the shape of a cross. The nave is flanked by 37 chapels, where churchgoers can worship some of the many Catholic saints.

A visit to Notre-Dame can be an overwhelming experience – and that is intentional. Medieval churches were designed to appear like small pieces of Paradise on earth, places where people could admire God's creation and also be reminded that he was the one in charge. In order to achieve this effect, Notre-Dame reaches high into the sky. At the main entrance, you are greeted by two square towers, 64 metres tall, and a facade decorated with statues of saints and gargoyles shaped like strange, scary monsters.

Inside the church, large columns rise up, meeting in pointed arches and high vaulted ceilings that seem like the sky itself. The structure is stabilized by exterior buttresses and flying buttresses – free-standing structures that lean against the building to keep the massive structure from collapsing under its own weight. Since the roof is carried entirely by columns, the outer walls can be decorated with large colourful glass mosaics, including the three round 'rose windows', the largest of them with a diameter of 14 metres.

In April 2019, the roof of Notre-Dame caught fire, which necessitated a huge restoration project. This is not the first time the church had to be restored, as it was also badly damaged during the French Revolution in 1789–1799. It was not until Victor Hugo wrote the novel about Quasimodo and Esmeralda, some 40 years later, that people in France appreciated the importance of the building. In his book, Victor Hugo

argued that after the turmoil of the revolution, religion and history were needed to rebuild France. This made Notre-Dame an important unifying national symbol.

To this day, Notre-Dame remains incredibly important to the French. This was clear from the great public interest when the building caught fire. In a very short amount of time, people all over the world had donated more than half a billion euros to the restoration. You certainly do not need to be a Catholic or French to appreciate the Parisian cathedral. With its Gothic architecture and heavenly light, Notre-Dame speaks to feelings that we all recognize, no matter where we are from.

Carcassonne, France.
Restored from 1853 with Eugène
Viollet-le-Duc (1814–1879) as the architect.

The Middle Ages recreated

'To restore a building is not to preserve, repair, or rebuild it; it is to reinstate it in a condition of completeness that never could have existed at any given time.'

This is how architect Eugène Emmanuel Viollet-le-Duc described the act of restoring a building or, as in the case of Carcassonne, an entire town.

Carcassonne is a fortified town on a strategically important hill in the south of France, where the trade route from Spain to the rest of Europe intersects with the trade route between the Mediterranean Sea and the Atlantic Ocean. Its powerful fortifications demonstrate how a key purpose of architecture has always been to offer protection against outside enemies.

The old part of town is surrounded by a double wall with 14 towers in the outer wall, dating from the 1200s, and 24 towers in the inner wall, which was built by the Romans when Carcassonne was part of the Roman province of Gallia Transalpina. Together with fortifications in the surrounding land, Carcassonne formed a strong military system that defended the French border region. Inside the city walls, which have a total circumference of three kilometres, there is a dense medieval town with narrow, winding streets.

During the 1800s, the town lost its military significance and fell into disrepair. It was soon destroyed because it turned into a sort of quarry, where people took stones to build new houses

47

elsewhere. But in the 1800s, when the Romantic movement rekindled the interest in ruins and medieval history, Carcassonne was rediscovered. In 1853, the architect Eugène Emmanuel Viollet-le-Duc was charged with restoring the town. He wanted to rebuild it exactly as it had looked during the Middle Ages. To achieve this, he carefully analysed which of the existing buildings deviated from the medieval style. He removed the houses that had been built in the space between the two walls and built new ones in what he believed was the original style.

In many cases, Viollet-le-Duc also added new elements of his own design. He wanted to achieve the 'condition of completeness' by using the ruin as a basis for creating a brand-new form. For example, he added a parapet to the cathedral because he was convinced that this building must have been part of the defences during the Middle Ages. As a result, the town we see today is shaped more by Viollet-le-Duc's vision of medieval architecture than it is historically accurate.

Thanks to the restoration that took place during the 1800s, Carcassonne is now a living example of a fortified medieval town. When you stroll through its streets, you feel that you have travelled back in time, and when you walk in the area between the city walls, it is easy to imagine how hard it would have been for an enemy army to break through.

Renaissance

Around 1400–1600

After the major calamities during the Middle Ages, the 1400s were a time of renewed optimism.

The Italian city of Florence was especially prosperous, and people had money to spend on art and architecture. Now, the Italians were keen to put the so-called 'dark ages' behind them. There was a strong movement to shape the future in the image of ancient Rome and Greece, which they considered the cultural peak of European history. Therefore, this new period has become known as 'the Renaissance', which literally means 'the rebirth'.

*On Architecture. Written around 25 BC by
Marcus Vitruvius Pollio (ca. 75–25 BC).*

Strength, functionality and beauty

Good architecture must be strong, functional and beautiful, as the Roman architect and engineer Marcus Vitruvius Pollio wrote in 35 BC in his book *On Architecture*. Remarkably, his point still holds true today, more than 2,000 years later. Naturally, architecture has to be strong and durable, so that it can stand for a long time. It also has to have a purpose, which is what separates architecture from other art forms. And, according to Vitruvius, a building without beauty is simply a building – it is not architecture.

On Architecture was almost forgotten until it was rediscovered in the early 1400s in a monastery in the Swiss town of Saint Gallen. A few years later, the German inventor Johann Gutenberg came up a with a new, efficient printing method. The timing was perfect, because now *On Architecture* could be printed in new, illustrated editions. As a result, Vitruvius's writings were widely distributed and studied by architects all over Europa.

With the renewed interest in ancient Rome and Greece, *On Architecture* became very influential during the Renaissance. It describes the ancient Romans' ideas about engineering, building materials and city planning. It also describes how architects should be educated.

One of the famous principles in the book is that the design of buildings should be informed by nature – more specifically, the natural human body. The brilliant artist and scientist Leonardo da Vinci played an important role in spreading this idea. In 1490, da Vinci created his drawing of the 'Vitruvian man', which has since become iconic. The drawing shows a man drawn inside a square, which is placed inside a circle. This symbolizes the role of humans as the centre of a harmonious and orderly world.

Vitruvius's book was a hit. And architecture would probably look very different today, had *On Architecture* not been rediscovered in Saint Gallen.

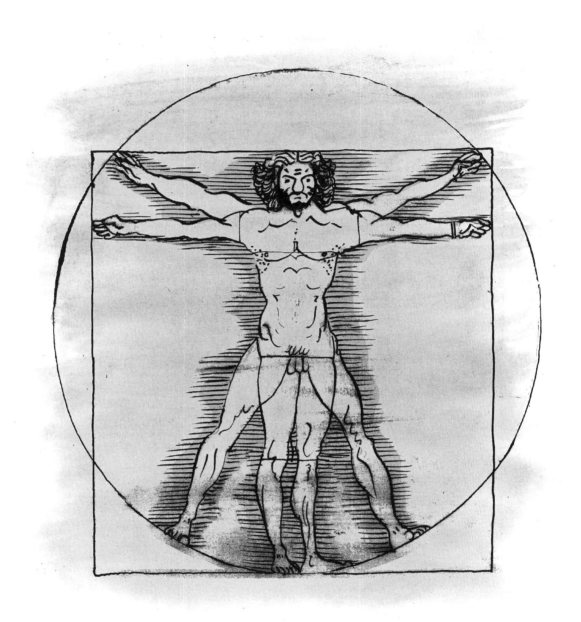

A dome of incredible beauty

The dome of the cathedral of Santa Maria del Fiore rises almost magically above the roofs of Florences as one of the great masterpieces of the Renaissance. It is one of the most beautiful sceneries in Italy. However, the dome is not only famous because of its beauty but also because of its unique construction.

The construction of Santa Maria del Fiore began in 1296. Florence was prospering, and the many wealthy merchant families wanted a new cathedral with a larger dome than the famous Pantheon in Rome (see page 22). Unfortunately, they had no idea how to construct such a dome, and even after the rest of the building had been completed, they still had not come up with a solution. Something had to be done, because a half-finished cathedral was an embarrassment, especially in a religious community such as Florence. In 1418, the town held a competition for the most beautiful dome design. The winner was Filippo Brunelleschi,

a goldsmith by training who was also a self-taught architect and had already designed several significant buildings.

Brunelleschi was facing a difficult task. Not only would the dome be built 55 metres above ground, it also had to be 45 metres in diameter with an octagonal (eight-sided) base. His solution was a brilliant construction that was capable of supporting its own weight during construction, which meant that scaffolding was not necessary. He used an ancient Roman method with a so-called herringbone brick bond – a pattern, where each layer of bricks could support the next layer, all the way to the top.

The finished dome consists of an outer and an inner shell, with stairs in between leading up to the viewing platform at the top of the cathedral. The eight curved sections of the dome are clad with ordinary red shingles, which might seem an odd choice for a cathedral of such great religious significance. But because the city roofs were covered with the same material, this established a beautiful link to the city and its citizens, not least the wealthy merchants who liked to feel a little closer to God.

*Villa Rotonda in Vicenza, Italy.
Built in 1565-1605 with Andrea Palladio
(1508–1580) as the architect.*

Villas in the countryside

During the Renaissance, most Italian cities were crowded, noisy and messy. Therefore, many upper-class families owned villas in the much calmer countryside. This had been common practice ever since antiquity, so the design of new villas was often inspired by classical architecture – and this was a style that architect Andrea Palladio excelled at.

One of Palladio's most famous designs is the Villa Rotonda. Sitting on a hilltop just outside the city of Vicenza, the villa has panoramic views of trees, meadows and forests, with a distant glimpse of the city on the horizon. Its design is rotated 45 degrees from the four compass points to make sure all the rooms get plenty of sunlight.

The villa has four identical facades, each with stairs leading up to a classic temple front. The explanation for the name of the building is found inside: each entrance leads into a lobby, and all lobbies open onto a large, round hall, called a 'rotunda'. This central hall is open all the way to the ceiling, where it is crowned by a dome with a window at the top. Through this window, daylight pours in, illuminating the interior first-floor balcony and the beautiful frescos. Like the facade, the floor plan shows an impressive degree of precision. The large stairs form a symmetrical cross, and the building itself is designed as a square with a circle in the middle. Palladio used these geometric shapes widely in his architecture, and like 'Vitruvian man' (see page 52), they reflect the Renaissance principle of harmony and order.

Palladio is undoubtedly one of the most significant architects who ever lived. His ability to understand and interpret the architecture of antiquity made him incredibly sought after in his time. After his death, his work continued to be highly influential. In fact, the architectural style of Palladianism is named after him – a style that was particularly popular in England and the United States during the 1700s. You can see the inspiration from Villa Rotonda in the design of the White House, the residence of the American President. When architects want to design a beautiful home, they might well borrow ideas from Palladio's Renaissance villas.

The stairway in the Laurentian Library in Florence, Italy.
Built in 1524–1571 with Michelangelo di Lodovico Buonarroti Simoni (1475–1564)
as the architect.

Michelangelo's unsettling stairway

The staircase hall leading into the Laurentian Library is quite small, but it is one of the most beautiful and intense spaces ever built. The room is square, measuring about 10 x 10 metres, but despite this precise geometry, it feels anything but static and stable. On the contrary, it has an unsettling quality – a sense of tension that you notice as soon as you enter. There is something unusual about this space!

The library was built to allow ordinary people to study the wealthy Medici family's valuable collection of books and manuscripts. It was designed by the great Renaissance artist Michelangelo, and with this building, he demonstrated that in addition to being a gifted painter and sculptor, he was also a brilliant architect.

Michelangelo used the familiar style of the Renaissance but without the harmony that was otherwise the norm. Instead, he distorted and exaggerated the forms, introducing a new style that became known as 'mannerism'.

The hall seems like a house turned inside out, with the four external facades facing in. The walls are smooth, white plaster with details in dark, grey-green sandstone. Everything is somehow 'off' compared with the rules of classical architecture. The pilasters taper in towards the bottom, and the half-columns do not belong to any recognizable order of columns. The columns are pulled back into deep-set niches, the corners are hollowed out, and the plastered walls push into the room. It seems to be the walls, rather than the columns, that carry the weight of the building.

This unsettling feeling is most dramatic in the sculptural stairway, which is divided into three sections. The bottom three steps in the middle stairway are shaped as large oval plates, and the polished steps appear to flow down and out, like cascading water. When you walk up the steps, you feel that you are being pushed backwards. All these built-in conflicts make the hall a unique experience that affects visitors both physically and mentally.

Old Stock Exchange in Copenhagen, Denmark. Built in 1619–1623 under Christian IV (1577–1648) with the brothers Lorenz (1585–1619) and Hans van Steenwinckel the Younger (1587–1639) as the architects.

Protected by four dragons

Christian IV is the best-known king in Danish history. He led a colourful life, enjoyed partying and drinking and had no less than 21 children. He was wounded during a sea battle and lost vision in his right eye. To this day, you can see his bloodied clothes from this battle on display at Rosenborg Castle in Copenhagen. But one of the main reasons he is remembered today is his passion for architecture and the many grand buildings he commissioned, including the Round Tower, Rosenborg Castle and the Old Stock Exchange.

Christian IV wanted to turn Copenhagen into a real metropolis. The money for his many building projects was to come through trade, so he needed a stock exchange to provide an attractive marketplace. The building was designed by the Belgian brothers Lorenz and Hans van Steenwinckel. Their

father had come to Denmark in 1578 with the goal of spreading the new popular style that we now know as the 'Dutch Renaissance'. Christian IV embraced this style so much that in later versions, it was even called Christian IV style. A key feature of this style is bands and sculptural ornaments in light-coloured sandstone that divide the facade into large brickwork sections. In contrast to the Italian Renaissance, the Dutch version included many colours, patterns and shapes, and the roofs were often made of copper or other metals.

The ground level of the Stock Exchange had market stalls that merchants could rent. The halls had direct access from the harbour front, and the upper floor with the large hall was accessed via an outside ramp on the west side of the building.

Christian IV liked to add striking features to his buildings, and the Stock Exchange is no exception. It has a tower with a spectacular spire that made the building visible to ships coming into the harbour. The spire is known as the Dragon Spire because it is shaped as four dragons with their tails twined together towards the sky. The dragons were believed to offer protection against enemy attacks and fire, and in fact, the building has survived several of the large fires that ravaged Copenhagen – some of them coming very close to the Old Stock Exchange.

Around 1770, the spire was in such bad repair that there were fears it might collapse. Back then, the preservation of historical buildings was not a high priority, so some suggested replacing the Dragon Spire with a low dome. Luckily, architect C. F. Harsdorff campaigned to maintain the original design. He argued that the spire was important for the overall look of the building as well as a key example of the use of Norse mythology. In 1771, the decision was thus made to reconstruct the Dragon Spire.

In 1857, when King Frederik VII sold the Old Stock Exchange, the contract included a clause requiring the new owners to preserve the building and its exterior, making it the first building in Denmark formally protected by law.

Baroque, Rococo and Neoclassicism

Around 1600–1850

In the 1600s, Catholic mass was held in Latin. Since only the best-educated understood Latin, the church had to use other means to tell ordinary churchgoers about the greatness of God. Therefore, they filled the churches with imposing decorations and dramatic paintings — a style that became known as the Baroque.

By the 1700s, people had had enough of the serious and emotional style of the Baroque. Now, they wanted things to be light, bright and playful! Noblemen built large Rococo-style mansions and palaces, where they could entertain each other and show off their wealth. But as the rich got richer, poor people grew more dissatisfied, which led to several bloody revolutions.

Now that the nobility was no longer popular or admired, no one wanted to design buildings in the old showy style. Instead, people once again turned to antiquity to find inspiration for a simpler, more human architecture. The result was Neoclassicism.

Although the styles developed in response to each other, they all have one thing in common: each in their way, the Baroque, the Rococo and Neoclassicism demonstrate how architecture can be used strategically as a way of expressing wealth and power!

San Carlo alle Quattro
Fontane in Rome, Italy.
Built in 1634–1667 with
Francesco Borromini
(1599–1667) as the architect.

A small building with a great impact

San Carlo alle Quattro Fontane is a very small church, but with its dynamic and moving features, it is also a Baroque masterpiece. The church has no straight angles and no sharp corners but is made entirely of complex forms, with curves and ovals weaving in and out of each other.

The church is named after the four fountains on the corners of the intersection where it stands. Its street front is divided into three sections and has a wavy design with niches used to display status. In the narrow street, it is difficult to view the building from a distance. It comes right up in your face, which makes the experience quite overwhelming.

Inside this fairly small church, your gaze is drawn up into the oval dome, which is topped by an oval window – an oculus. But instead of looking into the sky, you see a small space, a so-called lantern, that is filled with daylight. The ceiling of the lantern has a painting of a dove, symbolizing the Holy Spirit. When you see the dove from below, the daylight filling the lantern gives the picture a supernatural, religious effect.

The oval dome is covered by a three-dimensional pattern of hexagons, octagons and crosses. The pattern gets smaller towards the top, creating a sense of perspective that makes the dome seem taller than it actually is. Around the base, hidden windows let in daylight and make the dome look as if it is floating above the space inside the church.

Four rows of four columns each break the space up into the shape of a cross. Both the walls and the decorations have a neutral greyish white colour that makes the forms stand out. It is clear to see that the architect, Francesco Borromini, was also a sculptor. He had a masterly grasp of volumes and light and found inspiration in the forms of nature. That Borromini was able to produce these magical, intense experiences is amazing – especially here, in San Carlo, where he had so little space to work with.

Versailles outside Paris, France.
Built in 1661–1715 with Louis le Vau (1612–1670)
and Jules Hardouin-Mansart (1646–1708)
as the architects and André Le Nôtre (1613–1700)
as the landscape architect.

A residence fit for a Sun King

Versailles was built by the French King Louis XIV. Never one to underestimate himself, he was known as the Sun King. In his bedroom, he had a clock with the Greek sun god Apollo as a symbolic reminder than when he rose from his bed, the sun rose over France!

Naturally, Louis XIV needed a home fit for a king and began the renovation of a small hunting seat located in the Parisian suburb of Versailles. In 1682, he moved his court to Versailles, which in effect became the new capital of France. Several thousand nobles – and their servants – lived in the vast palace. It was expensive but necessary to live there, if you wanted to be close to the seat of power. The palace became the European hotspot for art, literature, theatre and music.

Three roads lead up to the palace. Before you reach the main entrance, you pass through three courtyards, each one narrower than the one before. The palace facade, which is more than half a kilometre long, is in the style of the French Baroque, later known as Louis XIV style.

Across from the palace were the royal gardens, which were every bit as important as the buildings – and just as the state had to follow the bidding of Louis XIV, so did nature! The surrounding marshlands were turned into a magnificent park with a striking central axis pointing into the endless landscape. Here, the Sun King could, very fittingly, watch the sun set in the west. Entire forests were planted, and the symmetrical paths were lined with statues, marble vases, pruned trees, sculpted hedges and flowers planted in geometric patterns. On this axis, a more than 1.5-kilometre-long canal is intersected by a second canal reflecting the sky. The Danish scientist Ole Rømer helped design the canal systems, using pressure to force the water into the many fountains, cascades and pools.

The famous Hall of Mirrors is 73 metres long and faces the garden. It is named after the 17 large mirrors on the wall across from large, arched windows. The reflections must have produced a dazzling effect at the gala balls hosted by the King.

Versailles took about 50 years to complete. While earlier royal castles served a defensive purpose and were built like fortresses, the purpose of the new palaces built with inspiration from the Versailles was to show off the occupant's power and prestige. In this regard, Louis XIV was very successful.

The city as a stage

In William Shakespeare's play *As You Like It*, one of the famous lines is,

'All the world's a stage, and all the men and women merely players'

The Rococo square Piazza di Sant'-Ignazio is certainly a stage where men and women come and go, like actors, and where the beautiful, curved buildings function as a stage set, designed to highlight the life unfolding on the square.

Piazza di Sant'Ignazio is situated in front of the Baroque church Sant'-Ignazio di Loyola in Rome, which was built about a hundred years before the square. The narrow streets in between the buildings make the large church seem even more impressive when you enter the square.

The piazza is shaped around three ovals and bordered by a string of curving facades. The buildings have very different backs, since they had to adapt to the irregular site. But towards the square, their facades form a symmetrical composition and a harmonious backdrop opposite the church.

The theatrical effects continue when you step inside the church. Here, Andrea Pozzo's paintings fill the church's vaulted ceiling. When you stand in one particular spot, an illusion of perspective makes it seem as if the church has a huge dome that continues all the way into the sky.

Piazza di Sant'Ignazio beautifully presents how Roman planners saw the city's streets and squares as some of the most important architectural spaces. As in the Shakespeare quote, they viewed the urban space as a setting for people to meet and socialize. The curved building facades make the residents an active part of the set and allow them to observe events on the square. Everyday life becomes a large interactive theatre performance full of people and life.

Nolli's map of Rome – La Pianta Grande di Roma. Drawn in 1736–1748 by Giambattista Nolli (1701–1756).

Oh, to be a cartographer

Giambattista Nolli was an architect and surveyor, but his masterpiece is not a building – it is his legendary map of Rome, 'the Eternal City'. He began this work in 1736 and did not finish until 12 years later, in 1748.

Nolli's map measures 176 x 208 centimetres and is incredibly accurate. For example, it is so detailed that we can see that the city's famous Spanish Steps are slightly crooked. All the ancient structures are drawn in black, while later buildings are drawn in grey, making the different periods easy to distinguish. This shows the city as a sort of palimpsest, which means that structures from different historical periods are placed on top of each other.

The most exceptional quality of the map is that it not only shows the city's streets but also the inner spaces of its public buildings. In this way, Nolli connects the churches and palaces with the city's squares and parks. He takes us inside the spaces where the Romans lived their daily lives, worshipped, traded and met with their neighbours.

The map itself is surrounded by pictures. In one corner, we see a woman wearing a papal hat. Behind her is the Capitol Hill, one of Rome's seven hills. In another corner, there is a picture of the goddess Minerva.

I became an architect, but as a child, I wanted to be a cartographer, and I always admired Nolli's map of Rome, which is one of the finest examples of cartography – the art of drawing maps. In addition, Nolli's map is also very practical and was used in Roman city planning as late as in the 1970s! In many ways, it is better than the maps you can get today from satellite photos and street views. With Nolli's map, you can let your imagination take you on a walk through the historical centre of Rome, which has hardly changed at all over the past 275 years. So next time you go to Rome, I recommend you to bring this map.

Amalienborg and Frederiksstaden in Copenhagen, Denmark. Built from 1750 with Nicolai Eigtved (1701–1754) among the architects.

God, king and country

Amalienborg is an unusual royal residence. The beautiful, open eight-sided square defines the palace complex and the surrounding district, which is called Frederiksstaden (Frederik's Town). Here, you can walk freely among the four palaces, which gives you the feeling that the royal residence is part of the city.

The Frederiksstaden district was built by Frederik V and designed by Court Architect Nicolai Eigtved. He organized the new district around the two streets Frederiksgade and Amaliegade, which intersect in the middle of the palace square. At the east end of Frederiksgade lies Copenhagen Harbour. This was where all

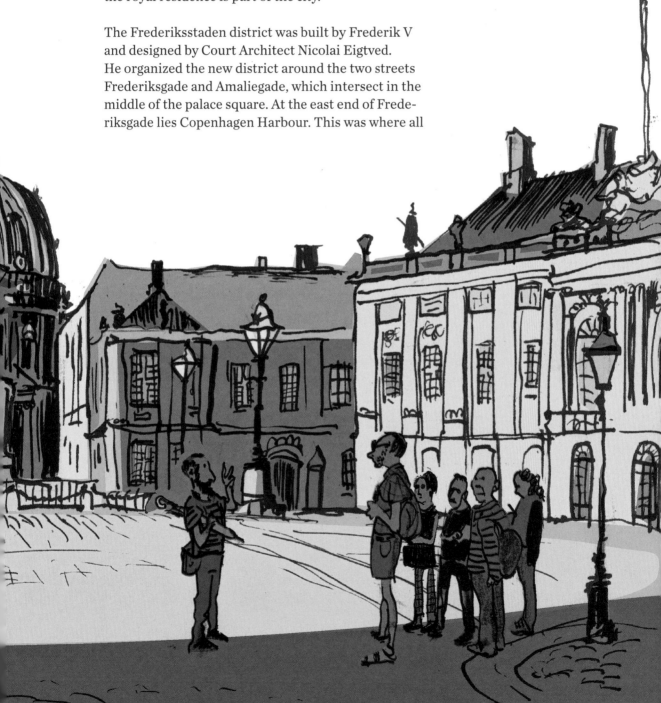

the big sailing ships docked when they returned with goods from faraway destinations. At the opposite end lies Frederik's Church, also known as the Marble Church, with its enormous, towering dome. In the centre of the palace square, the monarchy is beautifully represented by a statue of Frederik V on horseback set up in 1771.

On the outside, the four palaces were designed to look almost the same. The facades towards the square have a protruding central section – a so-called middle ressault – with tall windows, columns, a balcony and a decorated cornice. Each of the palaces is flanked by smaller buildings with gateways. The interiors, on the other hand, are more varied. Eigtved designed the impressive halls at Moltke's Palace with pastel colours, stucco ceilings, chandeliers and large paintings.

Amalienborg has been renovated several times. One of the most important additions is the colonnade from 1794, which links Moltke's Palace with Schack's Palace. It was intended as a temporary structure, so the columns were made of wood and painted to look like stone. However, the colonnade proved so popular that it is still here, and today, it is difficult to imagine Amalienborg without it. The latest major renovation was when Brockdorff's Palace was turned into a modern home for the then Crown Prince Couple, Frederik and Mary, in 2004–2010.

Amalienborg is one of Europe's most important examples of Rococo architecture, with its elegant architecture and intricate ornamentation. Originally, it was not intended as a royal residence but as separate mansions for four aristocratic families. That is probably why the palace square is open to pedestrians and cyclists. This makes Amalienborg a good example of Danish democracy, where the royals are close to the people. With the large church placed on one of the two main axes, you really get a sense that God, King and country are all present at once when you come here to celebrate royal events.

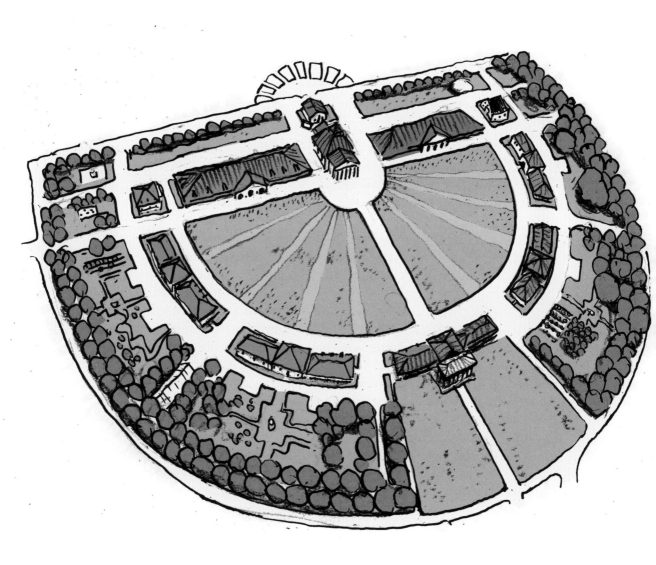

The factory as an ideal society

You probably think of salt as something we sprinkle on food. But salt has also been used to preserve food and to make glass, toothpaste, soap and paper. In France, salt was one of the main sources of income for the state, and the king was in charge of production.

In 1771, the architect Claude-Nicolas Ledoux was appointed as director of the Royal Saltworks in Salins-les-Bains. Here, the water in the underground had an extremely high salt content, but there was not enough firewood to build the large fires needed to extract the salt by evaporating the water. Ledoux decided to solve this problem by constructing a new saltworks near the forest of Chaux and dig a 20-kilometre-long canal to bring the salty spring water there. He had concluded that it would be simpler to bring the water to the trees than to bring the trees to the water!

When you see Ledoux's new saltworks, you might wonder if this really is a factory, because the architecture is so beautiful. The director's house is placed in the middle, with two large buildings on either side. Homes for the many workers are placed in a wide semicircle around the factory site. You enter through a monumental portal placed right in front of the director's residence. The entrance has eight large columns and an artificial salt grotto constructed of natural stones.

Claude-Nicolas Ledoux was one of the French 'revolutionary architects'. This may sound dramatic but is in fact just what we call a group of independent architects from the time around the French Revolution who wanted to simplify the refined architecture of the time. They preferred simple geometric shapes, such as the cylinders, spheres and cubes known from antiquity. The Royal Saltworks have a rustic, classical appearance with large unadorned walls and expressive detailing around windows and entrances.

Ledoux wanted to create a perfect architecture for a new era. In his vision, the harmonious, well-ordered factory became an image of the ideal society. The moral and happy life of the workers should be secured by providing family homes, communal kitchens and kitchen gardens as the setting for a strong community. This vision made Claude-Nicolas Ledoux a truly revolutionary architect!

Charlottenhof in Potsdam, Germany.
Built in 1829 with Karl Friedrich Schinkel (1781–1841) as the architect
and Peter Joseph Lenné (1789–1866) as the landscape architect.

Landscape and architecture in the spirit of antiquity

Charlottenhof was built for the Prussian Crown Prince to enjoy summers in Potsdam outside Berlin. The Crown Prince was an art lover with a passion for architecture, and since the architect Karl Friedrich Schinkel had given him drawing lessons, the two men planned Charlottenhof together. Some of the drawings were even made by the Crown Prince himself.

The interior of Charlottenhof is very colourful, but the summer atmosphere is especially striking in the building's most famous room, the fabulous tent room. Here, the ceiling and walls are covered with blue and white striped wallpaper and textile, so it looks like one of the tents Roman generals used in the field. Guests who spent the night here certainly got the full countryside experience.

When the project began, there already was a house on the site. The Crown Prince transformed it into this classical Greco-Roman villa since he was a big admirer of antiquity. The original roof was removed and replaced with a low pitched roof. The west-side entrance was designed as a monumental portal. On the east wall, the portal was repeated in the form of a vestibule with Doric columns facing the terrace and gardens. The Crown Prince Couple's bedroom was placed in a curved bay with a sweeping view of the gardens sloping down towards a pool to the north.

From outside, Charlottenhof looks as if it was part of an ancient temple complex. On the garden side, soil has

been built up to raise the garden above the park. Fountains, sculptures and pergolas with grapevines add to the feeling of being in the Mediterranean. It is clear to see that Schinkel found inspiration for Charlottenhof on his trip to Italy in 1817, where the ruins of the two Roman cities of Pompeii and Herculaneum were being excavated. Schinkel turned Charlottenhof into a sophisticated work of art, where the combination of architecture and landscape creates a stunningly elegant composition inspired by the spirit of antiquity.

Industrialization

Around
1850–1920

Over the course of the 1800s, many new inventions were made that changed the world forever. The most important was the steam engine: a motor that is powered by coal and steam.

Suddenly, steam trains and steamships made it easy to travel the world. Thanks to the invention of new farm machinery, farmwork required less labour, so many farmers moved to the city. Here, they found work in the new factories, where steam engine technology was used to mass-produce goods.

The new machines were made of steel and, as steel production became more efficient, the material also began to find its way into architecture. For example, steel was perfect for constructing the roofs spanning over the large factory halls.

These inventions brought industry into the cities, which became crowded with people and polluted by smoke from the factory chimneys. In fact, the development was so dramatic that this period is also known as 'the industrial revolution'.

Eiffel Tower in Paris, France. Built in 1889 with Gustave Eiffel (1832–1923) as the engineer.

An iron monument

The Eiffel Tower is one of the world's most iconic buildings and an incredibly popular tourist attraction. The tower stands more than 300 metres tall in the park Champ-de-Mars in Paris, where it was built for the Paris Exposition in 1889. The world expositions were recurring events where the wealthiest nations could showcase their new inventions and technological advances. The Eiffel Tower is therefore also an image of the optimism for the future that characterized the industrial revolution.

The Eiffel Tower was named after the engineer Gustave Eiffel, who designed the tower together with a team of architects. It is made of iron, which may seem like a base material for a monument, but here it is celebrated for its large potential with a structure that reaches for the sky.

The tower was constructed as a giant building kit. All the components were produced at a factory in a suburb of Paris and then driven into town on horse-drawn carriages. The various parts were then put into place and fastened with rivets. The builders assembled a total of 18,038 wrought-iron components using 2.5 million rivets.

No one had ever built anything of this size, and when the Eiffel Tower was finished, it was the tallest building in the world. According to Gustave Eiffel, this is why the tower has its characteristic flared shape, as he believed this was the best way to deal with the impact of the wind at this unprecedented height.

Originally, the tower was meant to be disassembled and removed after 20 years, but when it turned out to be useful as a giant antenna, it was left in place. During the First World War, the tower's powerful radio transmitters were used to block German communications, so after the war, it was seen as a monument to victory. Today, demolishing the Eiffel Tower would be unthinkable. It has become a Paris landmark and is illuminated every night in a festive display of lights.

A living organism of metal and mosaics

In an ordinary street in Brussels, there is an extraordinary house. Seen from outside, it might seem unremarkable. And yet – if you look a the railing on the balcony on top of the large bay, you can see how the metal bends and twists like a plant. When you step inside, you realize that the balcony was just a small indication of what to expect, as you will be blown away by the amazing interior with organic shapes everywhere – on the floors and walls and in the impressive stairway.

The building is Hôtel Tassel, and the style is called art nouveau. This style developed in Belgium and France during the late 1800s in response to mass production in the new factories that came with industrialization. Many European countries had similar movement, such as *Jugendstil* in Germany, *Skønvirke* in Denmark , and the Arts and Crafts movement in the United Kingdom.

Hôtel Tassel consists of three interconnected buildings: one towards the street and one towards the yard, both in brick and natural stone, and one in the middle constructed of steel with a large skylight flooding the interior with light. A large mirror at the top makes the room seem even larger than it is. Instead of a traditional floor plan with clearly defined rooms and corridors, the layout is based on large open spaces that flow together seamlessly. The heart of the building is the conservatory, where a sequence of bright, airy living spaces creates a light, open atmosphere.

The building's architect, Victor Horta, studied nature closely. With winding iron constructions, intricate mosaics and decorated lamps and furniture, he turned Hôtel Tassel into a sort of living organism. The elegant entrance section, with the lobby, conservatory and stairway, is an art nouveau masterpiece. Here, everything seems to be in motion, connected by swirls and curves in passages of fluid transitions. The stairs winding their way towards the daylight pouring in from above leave visitors stunned and overwhelmed.

Chrysler Building in New York, USA.
Built in 1928–1930 with William Van Alen
(1883–1954) as the architect.

A sophisticated skyscraper in shiny metal

In the late 1920s, New York developers were in intense competition to build the world's tallest skyscraper. At 391 metres, the Chrysler Building on Manhattan took the lead when it was completed in 1930. In addition to being tall, it was also one of the finest examples of Art Deco architecture.

Art Deco is short for 'art décoratif', and as the name suggests, its focus is on decorative qualities. The style was inspired by cultures all over the world, which were becoming more widely known through museum exhibitions, expeditions and archaeological excavations. Because of these influences, Art Deco contains inspiration from Africa and India, Mediterranean bronze-age cultures and Aztec and Mayan pyramids. The style also used the latest technological advances of the time and experimented with modern materials, including steel and aluminium.

The Chrysler Building was designed as the head office of the Chrysler car manufacturer and includes details that were borrowed directly from automo-

bile design. The facade decorations include elements from bonnets, wings and hubcaps. On the corners of the 61st floor, there are gargoyles shaped like bald eagles, the national symbol of the United States. The top 55 metres form a tall spire, which has made the building iconic. The spire consists of seven overlapping arches clad with silver-coloured stainless steel riveted into a sunburst pattern with triangular windows.

The lobby has a lavish decor with marble, zebra skin, sharkskin and lacquer! The dark and golden-brown materials alternating with shiny metal give the building's interior a very special muted and serious atmosphere. The lift doors have unique decorations, and the wall panels in the lift cars have geometric patterns of Japanese wood veneer, English hardwood, Oriental walnut and Cuban mahogany.

The building is constructed of steel frames assembled with almost 400,000 rivets. This method made it possible to build the skyscraper incredibly fast – the builders added about four storeys a week! Perhaps you have seen the photographs of construction workers in New York working several hundred metres up without a safety harness? Despite the height and the amazing pace, fortunately, no workers were killed in the construction of the Chrysler Building.

It only took one year before another building took its place as the world's tallest – the Empire State Building, also on Manhattan. However, the Chrysler Building is still considered one of the most beautiful and sophisticated skyscrapers in New York – perhaps in the world. There is something joyful and exuberant about the design. The combination of shapes, colours and materials is exciting. The building has a significant place in the city's skyline and history. It reflects both the industrial enthusiasm of the 1920s and the faith in 'the American dream'.

A tower that bends space and time

Since ancient times, statues have been used for architectural decoration, but the Einstein Tower is different. Here, the architecture itself is a sculpture. The Einstein Tower is an astrophysical laboratory designed to analyse the implications of Albert Einstein's theory of relativity.

The building consists of a tower with a dome that stands on top of a long underground section with a lab. Standing 15 metres tall, the tower almost seems to push out of the ground like a giant molehill. Inside the rotating dome, there is a large telescope that is connected to the underground lab via mirrors. In this way, the horizontal base and the vertical tower reflect the connection between earth and space.

The dynamic building almost looks as if shaped in clay. The windows seem to have been carved out of the soft mass, and the entrance section reaches out to welcome visitors. These living, flowing forms are strongly influenced by expressionism – an art movement in which artists represent their inner feelings in ways that can sometimes be a little scary. The design is architect Erich Mendelsohn's attempt at capturing the character of modern physics, in which space and time are no longer fixed entities.

According to Mendelsohn himself, his design sprang from the mystique around Einstein's universe, the idea arising as a 'sudden vision' which he then gave shape to. While he was sketching, he referred to it as both the 'mystical house' and the 'heavenly project'. As the story goes, he invited Albert Einstein on a tour of the completed building. Einstein remained silent during the tour, but a few hours later, he offered his understated opinion in a single, soft-spoken word: 'Organic.'

Looshaus in Vienna, Austria.
Built in 1909–1912 with Adolf Loos
(1870–1933) as the architect.

The naked building

GOLDMAN & SALATSCH

In 1913, the Austrian architect Adolf Loos wrote an essay titled *Ornament and Crime*. The title speaks for itself: ornamentation (decoration), which had always been an important element in architecture, should be banned. This view proved quite controversial. Shortly after the essay was published, he designed a very sparsely decorated building in Vienna, which led to one of the biggest scandals in architectural history.

Around 1900, Vienna was one of the wealthiest and most influential cities in Europe. This strong position included the field of architecture, especially with the newly established street Ringstrasse, where monumental and lavishly decorated buildings lay side by side. In this city, directly across from the Imperial Palace on the square Michaelerplatz, was the site of Adolf Loos's new, unornamented building.

The Looshaus, as the controversial building was called, was designed on behalf of a commercially successful tailor's business. The building was to contain a fashion shop, a workroom, a workshop and the owner's private home. In order to attract customers, the facade of the two lower floors would be clad with green marble and the entrance to the shop flanked by classical columns. On the upper floors, however, the facade was to be completely undecorated – just a clean, whiteish surface with square windows – a 'naked look' that the people of Vienna found indecent! Local news-papers described the building as 'the building without eyebrows', the 'wastebin on Michaelerplatz' and 'the height of moral depravity'. The opposition to the new building was so strong that the project was put on hold, and the client did not get permission to continue until they agreed to hang flower boxes under some of the windows.

One of the Viennese citizens who did not think highly of the Looshaus was the young Adolf Hitler. At the time, Hitler had ambitions of becoming an artist, and in 1911, he painted a picture of Michaelerplatz in which he deliberately replaced the Looshaus with a more ornamented building that once stood on the same site. Thinking of Hitler's later, horrifying acts, his criticism can almost be taken as a compliment.

When you visit the Looshaus today, it might be difficult to understand how the toned-down exterior could possibly cause so much trouble. To a modern observer, the building may even seem a little extravagant. But at the time and given the building's prominent location across from the Imperial Palace, the architectural design was considered an outrage. In fact, the 'building without eyebrows' was probably just ahead of its time. However, the scandal that surrounded the Looshaus helped sow the seeds for the modern style that later came to dominate architecture for decades.

Modernism

Around 1920–1970

In 1918, when the First World War ended, the view of the future was pessimistic. Industrialization had not just been a good thing – it had also made it possible to mass-produce machine guns, tanks and bombs. The war had led to fear and chaos, and now it was time to restore order.

Architects began to develop systems for everything, including writing new guidelines for designing homes that would support a healthy, structured life.

But not all the new systems were good. In the late 1930s, the Nazis attempted to introduce their own terrifying system, which was definitely not intended to benefit everyone. Ultimately, this led to the Second World War, where large cities were bombed and many people were killed.

When the war ended in 1945, life in the war-torn countries had ground to a halt. Many people had lost their homes and jobs. In order to build new homes, engineers developed new efficient ways of building with concrete, and in order to create jobs, factories went into overdrive.

Gradually, ordinary people were able to earn higher incomes and could afford to buy cars and therefore move to the suburbs. This was the image of the modern era: prosperity among the general population, single-family homes in the suburbs, wide roads and shiny, new tower blocks. Once again, the future seemed bright!

Bauhaus

Much of Europe was destroyed in the First World War, and it was in this ruined world that the German art school Staatliches Bauhaus (literally 'National House of Building') was founded. The school wanted to make architecture and design accessible to everyone – a revolutionizing idea, as it had so far only been something the wealthy could afford.

'Architects, sculptors, painters, we must all return to the crafts!' – as the school's director, Walter Gropius, described the purpose of the school. By bringing architecture, sculpture, painting, industrial design and handicrafts together under one roof, the school would make it possible for the students to be inspired by each other's work. In 1925, the Bauhaus moved to Dessau, where Walter Gropius designed the new school building. It became a prototype of modern architecture, which in 1932 was labelled the International Style. The building was completed in just 13 months, which in itself demonstrated the efficiency of the new and rational construction methods.

The building was completely without the ornamentation that had been part of architecture since the beginning of time. Instead, it had large, white fields of reinforced concrete and facades with large windows in iron frames. The flat roofs gave the building a clean geometric look. No one had ever seen anything like it!

Bauhaus was a place of free experimentation and was also known for its spiritual tendencies, avant-garde ballets and wild costume balls. But when the Nazis came to power in 1933, there was no room for all that, and so the school had to close. Since many of the teachers and students left Germany to go abroad, the closure helped spread the Bauhaus style to the rest of the world.

Today, we still associate clean lines, bright colours and clear-cut designs with this groundbreaking art school. And anyone studying to become an architect or designer will almost certainly encounter some of the methods from the Bauhaus that were so groundbreaking about a hundred years ago.

*Karl-Marx-Hof in Vienna, Austria.
Built in 1927–1930 with Karl Ehn (1884–1957)
as the architect.*

A working-class palace

Karl-Marx-Hof (Karl Marx Court) is the longest housing complex in the world. It is more than one kilometre long, and the tram that runs along the building has four stops before it has passed its full length! However, the building is not just interesting because of its size but also for its architecture and history. Karl-Marx-Hof was one of the first non-profit housing developments in Vienna. The client was the City of Vienna, and rent was cheap.

When the First World War ended in 1918, the Austro-Hungarian Empire collapsed, which led to widespread unemployment, poverty and famine. People lived in cramped conditions in small, unhygienic flats with little access to daylight and fresh air. A small house that barely had enough room for six people might in fact be home to as many as 40! There were no toilets, and people had to cook using dirty water drawn from unsafe wells. Under these conditions, typhoid and other contagious diseases were rampant, and many people died before their time.

This miserable situation gave rise to a strong labour movement, which called for change. In response, politicians tried to improve living conditions for workers, including building more housing. The Karl-Marx-Hof was designed as a shining example of good housing.

The building's 1,382 flats, measuring from 30 to 60 square metres, would be home to about 5,000 people. The small flats had a spartan design, but there were many communal facilities, including laundry rooms, baths, kindergartens, libraries and medical clinics. The structure itself only occupied about one fifth of the plot, so the rest could be turned into greenspace with gardens and playgrounds.

The building has striking, arched entrance sections, large balconies and towers with flagpoles. It is large and impressive. The City of Vienna even hired artists and artisans to create sculptures and decorations. A working-class palace to house the sort of ordinary people who had proudly helped build it.

However, in order to improve living conditions for the working class, the city had to raise taxes on the wealthy. This led to unrest and ultimately resulted in the Austrian civil war in 1934. In the clashes, the workers barricaded themselves inside the Karl-Marx-Hof, while the Austrian army, police and Fascists bombarded the building with small cannons until the workers had to surrender. Shortly after, the Fascists seized power in Austria.

Today, about one third of the population of Vienna still live in flats owned by the city. Non-profit housing has become an important part of the architecture and culture in Vienna. This sets a good example for other cities, where many flats are bought up by private companies, which raises rent prices so much that only the wealthy can afford to live there.

With its large red-painted base and decorations showing ordinary workers, Karl-Marx-Hof looks like a working-class palace. It sets an example for how a city can be designed to be welcoming to everyone.

The white style

The Swiss architect known under the byname Le Corbusier is one of the most significant designers in history. His buildings and ideas cannot be ignored. Even the way he dressed was noticed, and many architects began to wear 'Le Corbusier spectacles'. At an early stage in his career, he articulated five points of so-called 'modern architecture'.

The first point involved supporting the structure with 'pylons' (columns). This reduced the need for load-bearing walls, which also made the next three points possible: an 'open floor plan' for more flexible spaces, an 'open facade' allowing doors and windows to be placed more freely, and 'horizontal ribbon windows' that could wrap around the corners of the building. The final point was to construct a 'roof garden' on the now-possible flat roofs, providing an additional outdoor area equal to the building's footprint.

Villa Savoye clearly shows Le Corbusier's use of the five points. It consists of a white box raised up from the ground on thin, round concrete pylons. There is room for a car to drive in under the house, with stairs leading up to the first floor, which has bedrooms, living spaces, a dining room and a roof terrace. Large windows provide long views through the house and into the garden. Le Corbusier designed Villa Savoye as a so-called architectural promenade, where a ramp leads you through the entire building with architectural experiences along the way. The ramp ends in the roof terrace on the second floor, where sculptural screens provide sun shade and shelter from the wind.

Le Corbusier's architecture has become so famous that buildings such as the Villa Savoye have inspired a special category of modernism known as the 'white style'. His influence on the architecture of the 1900s cannot be overstated, and his expression continues to be copied by other architects.

A clearing in the woods

Villa Mairea is located in a clearing in a Finnish pine forest. Large window sections make the house transparent, and columns of wood and other natural materials inside the house gives you the feeling of standing among the pine trees in the forest.

The villa is a holiday home designed by the architect Alvar Aalto. It is L-shaped, with bedrooms in one leg of the L and living rooms in the other. The two wings come together in a large square living room with a fireplace, library, music room and conservatory. This central space is inspired by the 'stuga', a communal room in Finnish farms that, according to Aalto, can be traced back to the Sámi people in Lapland. The Sámi are a nomadic people, who used to live in tents and therefore only had a single room where they worked, ate and slept. In this way, Aalto interpreted local cultural heritage and gave it a new expression.

Alvar Aalto mastered classical architecture but designed buildings in the modernist style that was known as 'functionalism' in Northern Europe.

As the word reflects, it had a special focus on the function of architecture – both for the users and for society at large. But Villa Mairea is an example that function can be combined with a human approach. Aalto used materials and forms in a warm, playful way. The floors have different levels and are made of different materials. Curved shapes meet straight lines. Plastered exterior walls meet wood-clad ones. Wooden railings meet steel railings. And the fireplace is constructed of large natural stones.

This is a Finnish house, so of course, it has a sauna. The sauna is placed in a small, separate building in connection with an organically shaped outdoor swimming pool. When the sauna is on, the smell of the wood fire adds to the sense of being in the middle of nature and makes Villa Mairea a wonderful mix of Finnish folk culture and modern luxury.

The sound of falling water

Fallingwater – what a wonderful name for a building! And it is a fitting name. The building is dramatically built on rock ledges right above a waterfall, so the water appears to come rushing out underneath the house.

Fallingwater was designed by the famous American architect Frank Lloyd Wright. The building illustrates his idea of bringing architecture and nature together. Wright's work was often inspired by the American wilderness out west, where people had to adapt to the forces of nature. But with Fallingwater, we are in the heavily forested mountains in the eastern United States. The building literally grows out of its setting, as it is built from stones quarried close to the house. Terraces and staggered walls seem to be in motion under the large, flat roofs, balconies reach out to the surroundings, almost like horizontal rocks.

As in many of Wright's buildings, the fireplace is the heart of the home. Fire is a source of heat and food – basic survival. In front of the fireplace, he preserved the natural rocks that the house is built on. In other places, the floor is made of stones that have been polished to reflect the light like water. The large windows with red-painted frames pull the outside surroundings into the house and create a feeling that the interior space might just as well be outdoors. The bedrooms are small and low-ceilinged, which encourages the occupants to go into the living rooms or out on the balconies to take in the scenery.

When Fallingwater was completed, it was an extremely modern building that immediately drew attention. At the same time, the building also has an almost geological sense of age. It seems to grow right out of the rocks, as if it had always been there. The waterfall is not visible from every room in the house, but you can always hear what Frank Lloyd Wright called the music of the falling water.

Unité d'Habitation in Marseille, France.
Built in 1947–1952 with Le Corbusier (1887–1965)
as the architect.

A colossus on columns

Unité d'Habitation in Marseille is a giant concrete housing block. It is carried by huge columns that might make you think of enormous, grey elephant's feet. Like Villa Savoye (see page 106), it was designed by the Swiss architect Le Corbusier.

Le Corbusier disliked the single-family houses that had begun to sprout up around the cities. They took up too much space compared to how few people lived in them. Instead, he wanted to build efficient housing, what he called 'machines for living in'. With Unité d'Habitation, he wanted to create a 'vertical city', a development that grew upwards instead of spreading horizontally into the landscape. This would make it possible to use the land for greenspace.

The huge housing block contains more than 300 flats. It is 130 metres long, 21 metres wide and 56 metres tall. On every three floors, there is a large, interior street with entrances to the flats. The flats are on two levels and connect from the interior street to the floor above or below. Half-way up the building, there are two public floors with shops, function rooms, a restaurant, a hotel, laundry room and other communal facilities. In fact, if you lived here, you would never need to leave the building!

A visit to the rooftop of Unité d'Habitation is a stunning experience, not just because of the formidable view of Marseille and the beautiful landscape but also because the roof has communal functions for all the residents. It is like a landscape with a running track, a gym, a health centre, a day nursery, a kindergarten, a school, a playground and an open-air theatre.

The building's design was based on a system Le Corbusier called 'Modulor'. He developed Modulor in the spirit of Vitruvius (see page 52), basing a new set of measurements on the human body. He believed that this would make architecture both more beautiful and more functional. Like Leonardo da Vinci's drawing 'Vitruvian man', Le Corbusier also made a drawing to symbolize his Modulor system. His drawing – the silhouette of a man with one arm raised – is cast into the surface of the raw concrete at the foot of Unité d'Habitation.

The complex is one of Le Corbusier's most iconic projects and an important reference for any architect. It is an entire city in itself that combines private homes with excellent communal facilities. In this way, Unité d'Habitation shows Le Corbusier's social commitment and the potential of architecture to offer a better life for ordinary people.

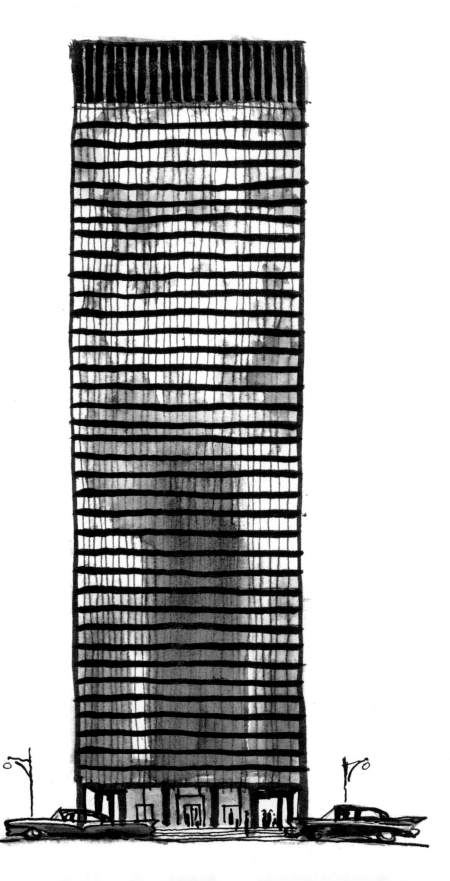

Seagram Building in New York, USA.
Built in 1958 with Ludwig Mies van der Rohe
(1886–1969) as the architect in collaboration
with Philip Johnson (1906–2005).

Less is more

'Less is more,' is the architect Ludwig Mies van der Rohe's most famous statement. By this he means that the simpler a building is, the stronger is its architectural expression. To understand how impactful a simple architectural design can be, we can look at his Seagram Building, a skyscraper on Park Avenue in New York.

When Mies was young, he wrote that he liked skyscrapers best while they were under construction, because then you could see the skeleton that supports the weight of all the floors. This is very clear in the Seagram Building, where the facades have a strict composition of vertical and horizontal metal ribbons.

Mies van der Rohe is also quoted for saying that 'God is in the detail', and this is certainly a concept he perfected in the Seagram Building. Here, simple forms are combined with expensive materials to make the building seem like an exclusive and elegant sculpture. The skyscraper can almost be seen as a giant geometric version of a classical Greek column with a base, a shaft and a capital on top.

The boxy shape was a little problematic, since in New York, all buildings over a certain height have to taper towards the top to let enough air and sunlight into the streets below. As a workaround, Mies van der Rohe pulled the building back from the street and established a new public space. This illustrates that architecture is not just about what we build but also, importantly, about what we choose not to build!

In many ways, the Seagram Building is the ultimate skyscraper and a modernist ideal. This means that it also lives up to a third important statement by Mies van der Rohe: that architecture can be defined as 'the will of an epoch translated into space'.

Sydney Opera House in Sydney, Australia. Built in 1959–1973 with Jørn Utzon (1918–2008) as the architect.

Between sky and earth

Few modernist buildings are known almost everywhere in the world. But with the Sydney Opera House, the Danish architect Jørn Utzon created one of the most iconic buildings on the planet. The building is not just a Sydney landmark but a symbol of the entire continent of Australia.

The Opera House is designed with a large, wide plateau with tall white 'shells' on top. The plateau contains the building's many practical functions, while the large shells contain restaurants, auditorium, the concert hall and the opera hall. It raises the building off the ground and projects it into the harbour with water on three sides. Here, people can arrive via a harbour-front promenade and ascend to the evening's performance by climbing a series of stairs that look almost like an artificial rocky landscape.

In his design of the shells, Utzon pushed the boundaries of what was possible at a time before computer-aided design. He simplified the construction process by drawing inspiration from the shape of an orange. By basing the design on a sphere, he was able to give the different shells the same curvature, which made serial production easier.

The outside of the shells is clad with a combination of matt and shiny tiles. This gives the building a beautiful white surface that varies with the light from the sky. Utzon called the white roof shells the 'building's fifth facade'. Like light-coloured sculptures, they spark associations to sails, the wings of birds or the cresting waves in Sydney Harbour.

Sydney Opera House seems at once brand-new and ancient – as if you were standing before the 5,000-year-old Great Pyramid of Giza in Egypt (see page 12). There is a feeling of timeless eternity when you stand on the large plateau under the white shells reaching upwards, somewhere between sky and earth.

St Peter's Church in Klippan, Sweden.
Built in 1962–1966 with Sigurd Lewerentz
(1885–1975) as the architect.

In a brick cavern

After he had not practised as an architect for many years, Sigurd Lewerentz was asked to design a church for the small town of Klippan in the south of Sweden. This was in 1962, and Lewerentz was an old man of 77. You may have noticed that this book is not about architects but about architecture. Often, however, the architect's personality and approach are an important part of the story of the building. This is especially true in the case of St Peter's Church in Klippan.

St Peter's Church is a strange building. It has an almost primitive feel, which is exactly what its admirers appreciate. Among architects, the story goes that Lewerentz spent three whole years on the building site instead of finishing the design in his studio. Together with the builders, he tried out different solutions and made sure everything was the way he wanted it. Sometimes, the builders had to pull down a wall if he was not happy with the result.

The church is correctly oriented in accordance to Christian traditions, with the altar to the east and the doors to the west, but pretty much everything else is nontraditional. The church itself is enclosed by an L-shaped building with a narrow street in between the two. This is where churchgoers arrive when they come to service. Lewerentz wanted people to make this ritual walk in order to get into the right frame of mind for the religious experience. Instead of the traditional long nave, the layout is based on a square. This lets the members of the congregation get closer to the altar and makes it possible to hold intimate services with chairs set up in a circle, as the early Christians did.

Every part of the building is made of the same local brick, so the entire room – outer walls, inner walls, floor, ceiling, altar and pulpit – has the same, dark colour. The nave's vaulted brick ceiling is supported by a large steel construction that looks like a huge cross. This combines the religious symbolism with the constructive function. The dark colours create an embracing, cave-like atmosphere.

In St Peter's Church, Lewerentz imposed a rule that the bricks could not be cut, which is otherwise normal practice. He kept a watchful eye to make sure this rule was observed in the laying of every single brick. The rule led to challenges in the form and construction of the building, so sometimes, he had to come up with tailor-made solutions. These solutions help give the building its unique character. He also told the bricklayers not to clean the mortar off the bricks in order to give them a rough texture with traces of the builders' work. The bricks are in contrast to the shiny windows, which are clamped onto the facade with just four mounts, so that the glass is invisible from inside the church.

St Peter's Church is small in size but a great source of inspiration. Here, form follows the religious rituals and symbols. The detailing, the materials and the light pouring in create a simple space inside the church that reflects a search for the simple things in life. It is a building created by an old architect who in his advanced age almost playfully demonstrated a lifetime's experience. The result is a strange and exceptional work of architecture that is almost vibrant with significance.

High-Tech, Postmodernism and Deconstruction

Around 1970–2000

Throughout architectural history, many competing ideas have always coexisted. Still, outlining the main trends remains relatively easy, at least until the modernism.

However, as we move into the second half of the 1900s, things become a bit more confusing. Suddenly, there are a lot of buildings going up, and architecture is influenced from every direction all at once.

Among other developments, technology became more advanced: American astronauts landed on the moon on 21 July 1969, and the first personal computers and mobile phones came on the market during the 1970s and 1980s. At the same time, there was a constant threat of nuclear war, while the hippie movement was pushing for a peaceful life in harmony with nature.

Perhaps the most general trend during the last few decades before the new millennium was that everyone found their own way to deal with a confusing world. Some tried to restore order, while others embraced the confusion and gave in to chaos.

Centre Pompidou in Paris, France. Built in 1971–1977 with Renzo Piano (born 1937) and Richard Rogers (1933–2021) as the architects.

High-tech from outer space

One might think that the Centre Pompidou looks like a factory. A giant technical installation, placed among the beautiful old buildings of historical Paris. The outside of the building is covered in brightly coloured ducts and pipes. Air-conditioning is blue, water pipes are green, electricity lines are yellow, and lift shafts and fire extinguishers are red. On the opposite side of the building, escalators cut across the 166-metre-long facade like snakes inside a Plexiglas tube. It is quite a sight!

The building is a modern cultural centre in Paris, designed by Renzo Piano from Italy and Richard Rogers from England. The centre houses a museum of modern art, a library, a centre for design and an institute of contemporary music. The architects wanted to create as much space inside the building as possible. That is why all the installations and load-bearing constructions, which normally take up a lot of room in modern buildings, have been placed on the outside. This means that all six levels are completely open, like factory halls, and that their layout can be changed depending on their use.

An important part of the Centre Pompidou is the large square in front of the building. Like the building itself, this square is named after the French president at the time, Georges Pompidou. As the escalators 'pump' people into the centre, visitors can look down at the activities on the square, with Paris as the picturesque background. On the escalators, they become part of the building's dynamic exterior, as they blend with the equally lively activities on the square.

The Centre Pompidou is a groundbreaking building and the essence of the technology enthusiasm of the 1970s. Architecture is turned inside out, and the technical 'guts' are laid bare in cheerful colours. Here, the machine becomes art in a futuristic celebration of everything high-tech.

Olympic Stadium in Munich, Germany. Built in 1968–1972 with Günter Behnisch (1922–2010) as the architect and Frei Otto (1925–2015) as the engineer.

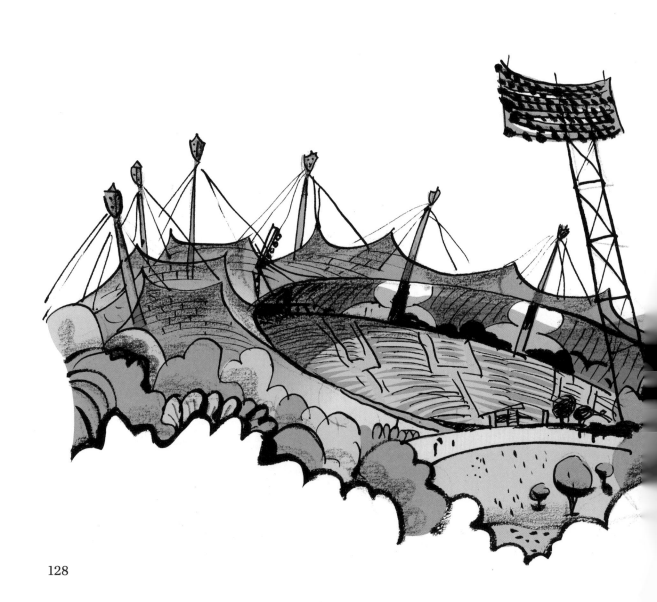

A weightless landscape of Olympic dimensions

Back in 1936, the Nazi regime under Adolf Hitler's leadership hosted the Olympic Games in Berlin. This is not something we remember with pride today. That is why it was especially important for the Germans to strike a very different note when they were to host the Olympics in Munich in 1972. It was important to avoid monumental buildings that were a demonstrative show of power, so the new Olympic stadium had a very different expression. Together, architect Günter Behnisch and engineer Frei Otto created a structure unlike anything the world had ever seen.

After the Second World War, rubble from the ruins of war had been dumped on a piece of land a few kilometres north of central Munich. The rubble formed a hilly landscape, which was chosen as new the site. The facility includes a stadium, a sports hall and an aquatics centre scattered across the large area. The man-made landscape was designed as an open park with lakes, hills and winding paths.

The buildings are partially underground, so only a third of the structures are visible. The sports arenas are tied together by a lightweight roof made of transparent plates hanging from a web of steel cables. The roof

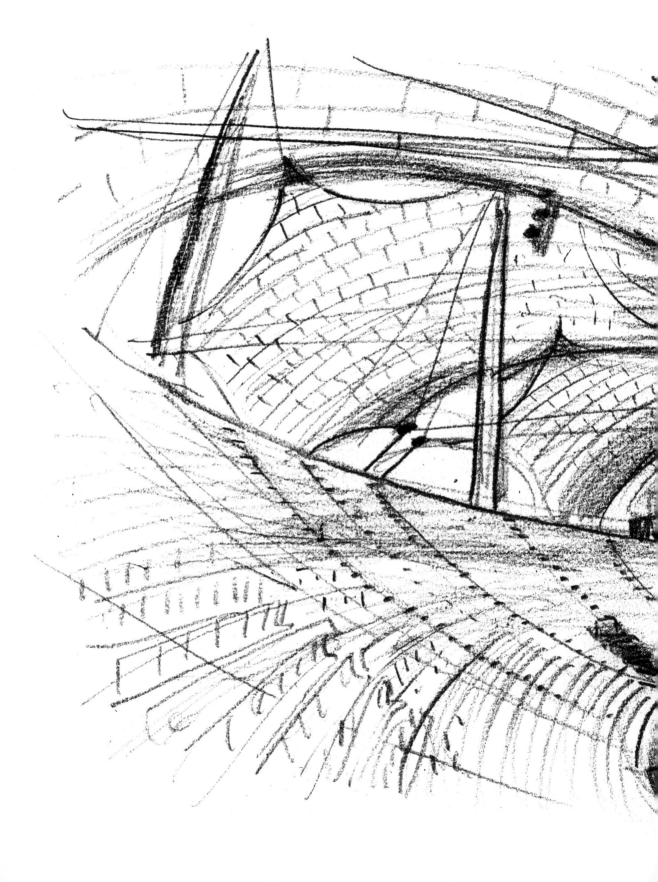

is supported by 36 poles and 12 giant masts, some up to 81 metres tall. Like a spider's web, this vast structure spans over much of the landscape and many of the buildings.

Munich is not far from the Alps, Europe's highest and longest mountain range, which inspired the architecture of the Olympic Stadium. The roof looks like a weightless landscape with sharp peaks, like a large crater with seating on the slopes. The lightweight tent constructions were revolutionizing for their time and still look modern today. This makes the stadium an icon of high-tech architecture – like nature in the form of art. You could say that Günter Behnisch and Frei Otto's design is an accomplishment that measures up to the athletes accomplishments in the stadium.

So did the architects manage to mark a break with the former Olympics hosted by the Nazis? The answer is a resounding YES! It is a great place to visit, and the Olympic park is very popular among the people of Munich, who use it for recreation and proudly show it off to visitors.

San Cataldo Cemetery in Modena, Italy. Designed in 1971–1976 and established in 1980–1988 with Aldo Rossi (1931–1997) as the architect.

The City of the Dead

In 1971, architect Aldo Rossi was in a serious car accident, but he was able to use this scary experience for a creative purpose. During his long hospital stay, he found the inspiration to design the San Cataldo Cemetery. He called the project 'The City of the Dead'.

The cemetery consists of clean geometric shapes laid out in a large rectangle. At one end, there is a large, red cube. At the opposite end, he designed a tall, conical tower, and in between he added a triangular complex of parallel buildings. From above, Ret til: it would look like ribs attached to a spine, and like the broken bones in Rossi's own body, the buildings were to be assembled into an architectural skeleton.

The buildings contain graves and memorials to people who were victims of war. The large, red cube has no ceiling, floors, windows or doors, only a thick wall with square openings. Inside, the urns with the ashes of the dead are kept in small, four-sided openings that the visitors can reach by climbing simple metal steps.

In his book *The Architecture of the City* from 1966, Aldo Rossi describes the historical city as a living organism, where different periods leave their imprints, generation after generation. He writes that architecture has developed certain forms and ideas that are repeated throughout history and which have become recognizable types in people's awareness. Based on this theory, Rossi searched for a timeless expression, which is clearly expressed in the simple geometric shapes of the San Cataldo Cemetery.

Even though the cemetery may look simple, its meaning is complex. Aldo Rossi has been described as a poet who happened to become an architect! This cemetery is a masterly example of Rossi's poetic expression. As Rossi explained, he designed it to look like an empty house that the living could fill with their memories of the dead.

Neue Staatsgalerie in Stuttgart, Germany.
Built in 1977–1984 with James Stirling (1926–1992)
as the architect.

An architectural collage

A common view of history is to see any stylistic period as a reaction to the previous period. In this way, post-modernism can be seen as a reaction to modernism and its strict rules, which some saw as inhuman or elitist. In the early 1970s, historical motifs were virtually shouting to be allowed back in an encounter with modern expressions. The art museum Neue Staatsgalerie set the tone for this development and, in principle, contained all the characteristics of postmodernism.

At its core, the Neue Staatsgalerie is a classical building, a heavy structure clad with robust stone plates. But this material clashes with the museum's many colourful details. The main entrance has a canopy in blue steel. Pink and blue steel tubes are used to guide visitors through the building, and large, flowing glass facades on the front of the building are framed by heavy green profiles. The result is a unique look that combines historical elements with brightly coloured modern design elements.

In the centre of the museum, there is a rotunda, a circular courtyard, which was also a feature in Renaissance architecture and in museums from the 1800s. Here, we find traces of architectural history, such as classical columns and arches. In the passage that winds its way up along the wall, we encounter more references from ancient times, classical antiquity and the Gothic, all the way up to modernism. This promenade turns the building into a fluid architectural landscape that you can experience without buying a ticket to the museum.

Inside, the exhibition halls are arranged in a U-shape, similar to the layout at the Alte Staatsgalerie, the older art museum next door. The halls are placed in a sequence with long views through the connecting doors. This layout is called an 'enfilade' and was very popular during the Baroque.

With its many references, the Neue Staatsgalerie is an architectural collage. It can be seen as a study of historical forms and a celebration of architecture as a discipline. The many styles and elements have been reinterpreted in a new and exciting way. This is post-modernism at its best!

Jewish Museum Berlin, Germany. Built in 1989–1999 with Daniel Libeskind (born 1946) as the architect.

Empty space

During the Second World War, the Nazi regime murdered six million Jews, many of them their fellow German citizens. The Jewish Museum Berlin, designed by the Polish-American architect Daniel Libeskind, commemorates the victims of this inconceivable cruelty, now known as the Holocaust.

The museum consists of an existing Baroque palace and Libeskind's new building, connected by an underground passage. Seen from above, the new building has a dramatic zigzag shape perhaps resembling a flash of lightning or an asymmetrical, broken Star of David, the symbol of Judaism. The windows are sharp slits, as if a knife had sliced into the shiny metal facade.

The new building looks very striking from outside, but it is the interior that really tells a story! Here, Libeskind has created a series of empty spaces – voids – to represent the many murdered Jews. The visitor encounters these empty spaces throughout the museum without ever being able to enter them. They are only experienced through

cracks and openings where you faintly glimpse the names of the dead, written on the walls. At one place in the building, visitors can walk through a steel door and into the 24-metre-tall Holocaust Tower: a cold, dark, empty room where you can remember the victims. When the steel door slams shut behind you, you are left inside the shaft, as if you were standing at the bottom of a tall chimney.

Libeskind calls the design concept 'between the lines', because the building's ground plan is based on two lines representing two different timelines. One is a straight line divided into many fragments, the other a winding line that continues indefinitely. It is the interaction between these two that gives rise to the disconnected void that runs through the building.

The museum is one of the most distinctive examples of Deconstructivism, an important architectural trend in the late 1900s. The point of Deconstructivism was to take all the building's components apart and then put them back together in new, experimental ways. In the Jewish Museum Berlin, Libeskind also takes the notion of 'rationality' apart, because he thinks 'rationality' has been used as an excuse for war and killing. Instead, he wanted to create a museum that is irrational, illogical and perhaps even confusing.

To Libeskind, architecture is a language of metaphors and references. His drawings for the Jewish Museum Berlin are full of notes about literature, history, philosophy and music, which flow into the deconstructed design as a complex understanding of Berlin's Jewish history.

The New Millennium

2000 to now

How do you think our time will be remembered?
This is difficult to predict, as we can still see
traces of various architectural developments
from throughout history when we look around.

Even today, some buildings are designed to
show off power and wealth. We still discuss how
much ornamentation is appropriate for a facade.
And it is still unclear whether it is better to try to
restore order or to embrace chaos.

One thing that does characterize our time is that for many people, the world is getting much smaller! In theory, it is possible to be a British architect working in a studio in Japan while designing buildings in Brazil.

Globalization is making it easier to exchange ideas, which is great for development. But it can also make it harder to tell the difference between a skyscraper in Shanghai and a skyscraper in Dubai.

The most important factor influencing architecture in recent years is our growing awareness of the harmful climate effect of too much construction. There are many opinions about what we should do instead. Perhaps we should stick to local, traditional materials. Or maybe we should stop constructing new buildings and be better at maintaining the ones we have, so they do not have to be demolished.

Either way, there is a growing agreement that something needs to change, and more and more architects are working on finding the best solutions. Young architects in particular are very active. After all, it is their future that is at stake.

MAXXI in Rome, Italy.
Built in 1998–2010 with
Zaha Hadid (1950–2016)
as the architect.

Computer architecture

The American musician Lou Reed once said that his song-writing changed when he bought a computer. When he wrote songs on a computer, the machine influenced the song's poetic content and overall artistic expression. Architecture also changed fundamentally when architects began to make designs on a computer instead of drawing by hand. One excellent example of this is the modern art and architecture museum MAXXI in Rome, which was designed by the Iraqi-born architect Zaha Hadid. Without a computer, it would not have been possible to design, or even to imagine, a building like MAXXI.

Before the invention of computers, architects drew everything by hand. This means that spatial, three-dimensional shapes were created on flat, two-dimensional paper. To see something in three dimensions, architects could build a model in cardboard and wood, which was a slow process. The new computer programs made it possible to draw directly in 3D and instantly see how the entire building changed with every minor adjustment. Computers could also generate shapes based on mathematical formulas. Suddenly, it was much easier to design complex buildings, and Zaha Hadid took full advantage of these new possibilities!

Seen from outside, MAXXI may seem like a confusing combination of building parts overlapping in fluid motion. When you enter the large lobby, the complexity becomes even more striking. As in a labyrinth, openings and floating black stairs lead to the many different departments of the museum. The steps are made of metal grids, so you can look straight through to the floors below, which can be a little scary if you suffer from a fear of heights.

The curving walls form a fluid sequence of spaces. Here, visitors are supposed to experience architecture by moving through them. In some places, the walls bulge out to form exhibition spaces in contact with the surrounding city. In other places, the corridors feel like narrow tubes that direct you forward. You might worry that the surprising forms would steal all attention. But the combination of natural light and smooth, white concrete creates a neutral background that highlights the art.

This book is not about architects but about architecture. However, if you examine the works of architecture I have included, historically, they have predominantly been created by men. Fortunately, this has changed, and nowadays, women are just as influential in the world of architecture. Zaha Hadid was one of the first women to step into the limelight as an internationally acknowledged architect, and you can find her innovative works in many places around the world.

Quinta Monroy in Iquique, Chile. Built in 2003–2004 with Alejandro Aravena (born 1967) and ELEMENTAL as the architects.

Half a house for a whole family

In the 1960s, about a hundred poor families settled in Quinta Monroy, an area in the city of Iquique in northern Chile, where they lived illegally for more than 30 years. When the authorities wanted to legalize the area, the land had become so expensive that the families could not afford to stay. This meant that they were at risk of being evicted and displaced to the margins of the city, far away from jobs, education and healthcare facilities. Isolating marginalized citizens in this way can lead to social conflict and disadvantaged

neighbourhoods. So when Alejandro Aravena and his architecture firm ELEMENTAL was hired to design the new Quinta Monroy, their top priority was to enable the current residents to stay. But how to achieve that?

In order to make the plots affordable, they had to put the houses close together, so they chose to build terraced houses. It was also important to use durable materials, so that the buildings would not lose value over time. In order to afford quality materials, the architects came up with a clever solution. Instead of building a whole house of mediocre quality, they built half a house of good quality – for the same cost! Over time, the residents could then add the other half themselves when they could afford it, which would increase the value of the house.

Quinta Monroy shows that architecture can help solve social problems and overcome poverty. With this goal, the role of the architect has expanded. Today, architects work closely with politicians, lawyers, scientists, local authorities and clients, but they also work with the users. This helps the people who are going to use the architecture feel a sense of ownership. Quinta Monroy demonstrates why the architects make the extra effort: they want to make the world a better place to live.

Wall House in Auroville, India.
Built in 1997–2000 with Anupama Kundoo
(born 1967) as the architect.

An experimental sustainability lab

Wall House is not just the architect Anupama Kundoo's private home, it is also her experimental lab for sustainable construction. The house has clear, simple forms but is also complex. It is organized around a long, narrow room with a vaulted roof and a number of alcoves and projecting sections for different purposes. Along the outer walls of the house, there is a four-metre-wide, vaulted overhanging roof. The living spaces are open to nature, and wide steps inside the house continue smoothly into the garden. It is hard to tell where the inside ends and the outside begins.

The walls are made of traditional Achukkal bricks, a type that was once used all over Tamil Nadu, the southernmost state in India. It is a flat, thin brick with a characteristic red colour that creates a warm atmosphere. The brick is also sustainable, because it is durable and does not require much energy to make. Local potters helped build the roof. The vaulted ceiling

consists of clay tubes, and clay pots are cast into the flat slabs between the floors. The hollow space inside the tubes and pots reduce the amount of concrete that is needed.

Because of its construction, the house is well suited for the hot, humid climate and uses very little energy. A solar-cell system produces electricity, and water is provided by a solar-powered pump and a solar water heater. The tall ceilings increase the natural ventilation, with windows and other openings letting in fresh air and lots of daylight. On one side of the building, there are slatted windows made of local mango wood. On the other side, towards the green landscape, there are pivoting perforated screens that create beautiful patterns of light and shade. A transparent wooden mesh offers views of the sunset in the west.

The house is a mix of high-tech and low-tech, machine-made and handmade. By using ancient techniques carried out by unskilled builders, Kundoo supports the local community and reduces her climate impact. This has made Wall House a source of inspiration for architects wishing to design sustainable buildings.

*Allmannajuvet in Sauda, Norway.
Built in 2016 with Peter Zumthor
(born 1943) as the architect.*

Buildings with insect legs

Allmannajuvet is the name of a magical place in the Norwegian mountains south-west of the Hardangervidda mountain plateau. Here, the Storelva river runs through a remote, forested landscape. An impressive road winds its way along the river leading to an area where zinc was mined from 1881 to 1899. While the zinc mine was in operation, it was an important source of income for the local community. This was before the Norwegian oil fields were discovered and Norway had yet to become a wealthy country.

Scattered throughout the landscape are three small buildings that make the area accessible to visitors and tell the story of its industrial past. The buildings blend discreetly into nature but also have a striking apperance and placement. When you arrive, you can sense that there is something going on here, like a secret that is beginning to reveal itself.

The site is on one of the new Norwegian Scenic Tourist Routes, which run through areas with unique landscapes, along coasts and fjords, mountains and waterfalls. As with the visitor facilities

at Allmannajuvet, the architecture along the routes often becomes an attraction in itself.

The Allmannajuvet project was designed by the Swiss architect Peter Zumthor and consists of a museum building, a café, toilets, a car park, trails and stairs. The simple buildings were inspired by the mining operation. Along the car park, there is an impressive, curved wall in natural stone that rises 18 metres above the rushing river. The buildings look like large, insect-like creatures balancing on the rocks on long legs, clinging to the surface as if they had suckers on their feet. The buildings are made of wood, and inside, the walls are lined with cloth and painted in a dark colour, which gives the space a cave-like feel.

Before Peter Zumthor established his own architecture studio, he worked with listed buildings for many years as a civil servant. This experience still influences his work, and his architecture seems untouched by fleeting trends. It has a sort of eternal character – a sense of permanence.

Allmannajuvet is an example of Zumthor's ability to create movement through landscapes and buildings. With great respect for the site and local cultural heritage, he reduces the architecture to the essentials and creates a very special atmosphere. This is timeless architecture that is both modest and bold. It has a clear poetic dimension that speaks to all our senses.

Neues Museum in Berlin, Germany.
Originally built in 1843–1855 with
Friedrich August Stüler (1800–1865)
as the architect. Restored and trans-
formed in 1999–2009 with Julian Harrap
(born 1942) and David Chipperfield
(born 1953) as the architects.

The qualities of ruins

During the Second World War, the Neues Museum in Berlin was badly damaged by bombs. In the early 1990s, when I worked in Berlin, you could still see bullet holes in many of the buildings in the former East Berlin after the street fights in 1945. And inside the ruins of the Neues Museum, there was almost a small wood of self-sown plants.

The Neues Museum in Berlin was originally designed by the architect Friedrich August Stüler and construct-ed in 1843–1855. In 1997, the English architects Julian Harrap and David Chipperfield won an international competition to rebuild the museum. Since 1961, Berlin had been split in two, but in 1989, the Berlin Wall came down, and soon after, East and West Germany were reunited. This was no easy process, and the museum became an important national symbol of the reunified Germany.

The reconstruction required in-depth understanding of the building's history and ruined structure. Every room was studied with archaeological precision to document the original details. The restoration was innovative, as it did not attempt to build a perfect copy of the original building nor a modern extension that would contrast it. Instead, the architects preserved everything they possibly could and only added new elements where it was necessary. This highlighted the qualities from the full lifespan of the building – including the years when it was left as a ruin.

In the staircase hall in the middle of the building, this approach is clearly visible. The monumental stairway has been rebuilt but in a simplified version in a mixture of concrete and white marble. The brick walls still look like a ruin with traces of the frescos and ornamentation that were destroyed during the war.

Through a dialogue between the old and the new, the museum forms a new, third structure. Harrap, who specialized in restoration, tidied thing up and highlighted the building's history, while Chipperfield, who specialized in architecture, added a new layer to the existing structure. The two approaches came together perfectly to make the Neues Museum an image of Berlin's complex past.

Startup Lions Campus in Turkana, Kenya. Built in 2021 with Francis Kéré (born 1965) as the architect.

Inside a termite mound

Once, when I was travelling in Kenya, I had hitched a ride on the back of lorry in a desert landscape. It was a blisteringly hot day, so I went for a swim when I came to Lake Turkana. I had heard that the lake was home to more than 10,000 crocodiles, but according to the locals, they stayed in the colder waters in the middle of the lake. The banks of this lake are now the site of Startup Lions Campus, designed by architect Francis Kéré.

Startup Lions Campus is a college consisting of five connected buildings with classrooms, workshops and housing for 300 students. The buildings have roof terraces with great views of Lake Turkana. The college also has tall, earth-coloured towers inspired by termite mounds!

Termites build their mounds from soil mixed with saliva and excrement. When the mixture dries, it becomes as hard as rock. These termite mounds can be up to seven metres tall, but underground, they are even bigger, as this is where the termites live in a complicated network of tunnels and chambers. What we see above ground is just the insects' climate control units, which regulate the underground temperature and air humidity.

Like these termite mounds, the earth-coloured towers at Startup Lions Campus provide ventilation. As hot air rises up, fresh air is pulled in through low-set openings in the walls, with no need for electricity.

Startup Lions Campus offers free education to make it easier for young locals to find work and earn a living. Francis Kéré grew up poor in Burkina Faso, and even though he has become a world-renowned architect, he has not forgotten where he came from. He actively works to improve life for countless people in places that sometimes seem to have been forgotten by the world. Kéré once said that 'If we learn to build with local materials, we have a future'. That is exactly what he did at Startup Lions Campus. The wind towers are a beautiful addition to the landscape and a celebration of the local natural setting.

Name index

Glossary

On the following pages, you can find explanations of the words marked in red in the text.

Basic geometry

A proportion is the relationship between two measurements. For example, the proportion between the sides of a square is 1:1, because the sides are the same length. For the rectangle surrounding this text, the relationship between the two sides is 9 x 4. This is the same proportion that is found throughout the Parthenon (see page 22).

Sphere

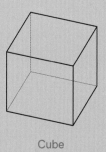

Cube

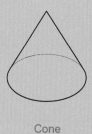

Cone

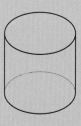

Cylinder

When two forms are parallel, they are side by side and point in exactly the same direction.

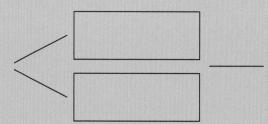

An axis is a straight line that you can draw directly through something, for example a garden.

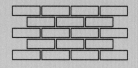

A brick bond is the pattern bricks are laid in. On the left is a typical brick bond, on the right, a herringbone bond.

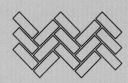

Temples in antiquity

The classical order of columns is a way of categorizing columns based on their shape. The three best-known categories are shown below.

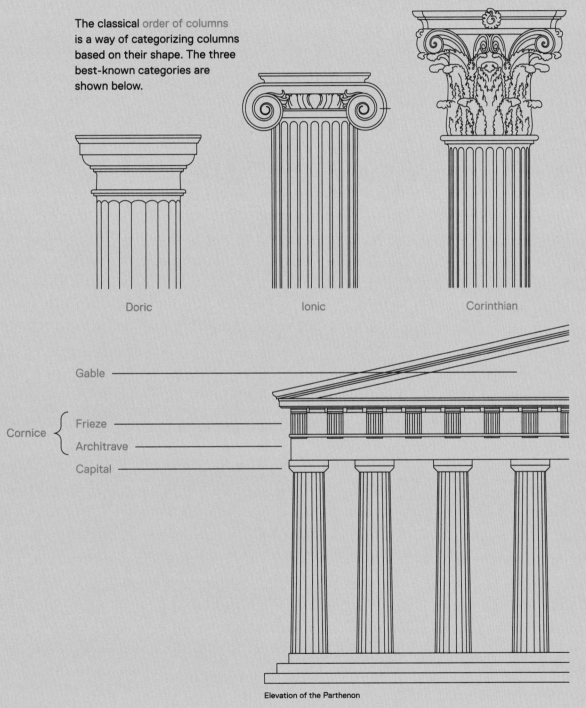

Doric

Ionic

Corinthian

Gable

Cornice
- Frieze
- Architrave

Capital

Elevation of the Parthenon

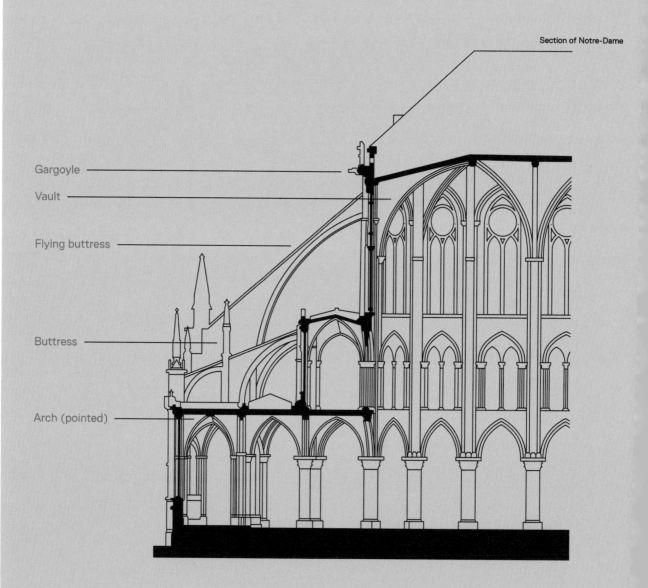

Section of Notre-Dame

Gargoyle

Vault

Flying buttress

Buttress

Arch (pointed)

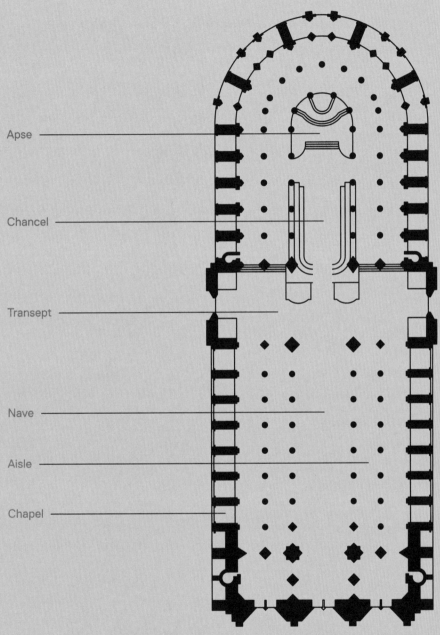

Apse

Chancel

Transept

Nave

Aisle

Chapel

Plan of Notre-Dame

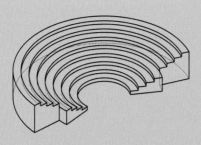

Amphitheatre
A type of theatre in antiquity where the spectators are seated on steps around the stage.

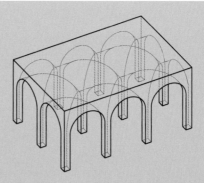

Arcade
Rows of columns with vaults above.

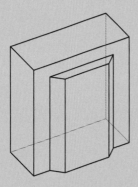

Bay
A part of a room that extends beyond the main perimeter of the house. Often with windows.

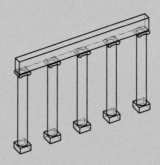

Colonnade
Rows of columns supporting a roof or a canopy.

Minaret
A slender tower used in Islam to call worshippers to prayer.

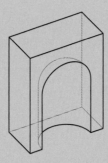

Niche
A recess in a wall. Often used to display a statue.

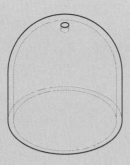

Oculus

The word 'oculus' means eye and is used to describe the hole at the top of a dome.

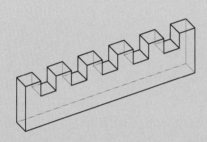

Parapet

A protective wall on a fortress. Parapets often had embrasures (openings), so the defenders could look out and shoot at attackers.

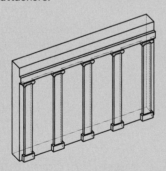

Pilaster

A decorative column that is partially embedded in the wall.

Lorem ipsum dolor sit am
consectetuer adipiscing e
diam nonummy nibh eui
tincidunt ut laoreet dolor
magna aliquam erat vol
wisi enim ad
nostrud

Palimpsest

A palimpsest is a piece of reused parchment where the remnants of previous texts can still be deciphered beneath the new writing.

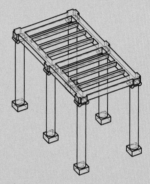

Pergola

An open structure with a roof over it on which climbing plants can grow.

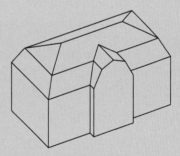

Ressault

A ressault is a projection in a facade, often seen in baroque buildings.

Heights

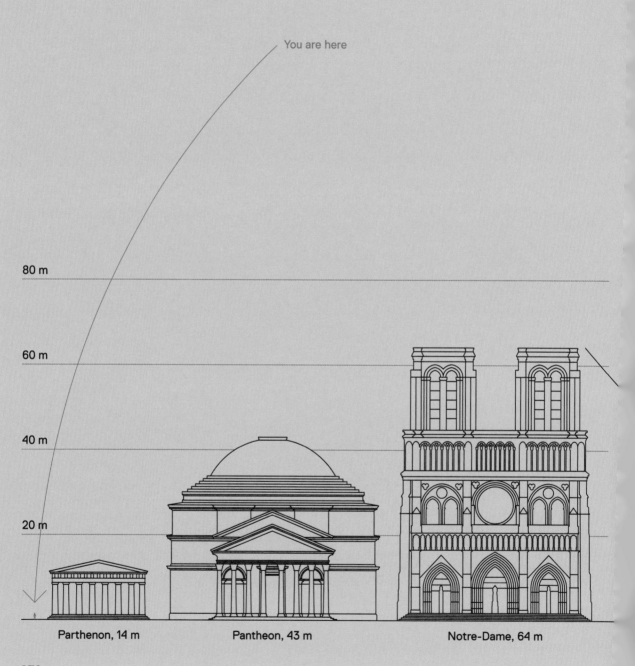

You are here

80 m

60 m

40 m

20 m

Parthenon, 14 m

Pantheon, 43 m

Notre-Dame, 64 m

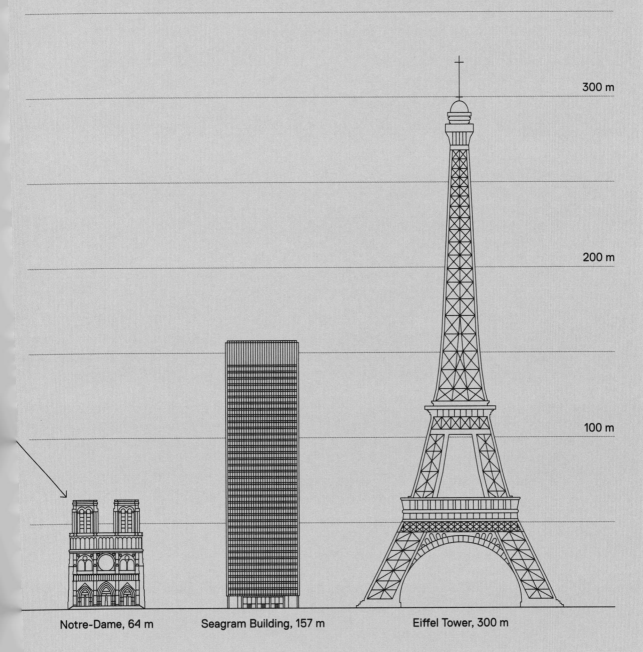

The world's tallest building, 823 m

400 m

300 m

200 m

100 m

Notre-Dame, 64 m   Seagram Building, 157 m   Eiffel Tower, 300 m

**The Little Book of Architectural History
for Children and Curious Grown-Ups**

Illustrations: Claus Nørregaard
Cover and graphic design: Søren Damstedt, Trefold
Concept: Peter Michael Hornung
Publishing editor: Nicholas Jungblut
Translation: Dorte Herholdt Silver
Copy-editing: Cornelius Colding

The book is typeset in Replica and Chronicle Text
Paper: 150 g Munken Lynx Rough
Printing: PNB Print
Printed in Latvia 2024
1st edition, 1st print run
ISBN: 978-87-92596-60-4

Quotations:
Page 47: Eugène Viollet-le-Duc: *On Restoration*. Sampson Low,
Marston Low, and Searle, 1875.
Page 73: William Shakespeare: As You Like It. In *The Complete
Works*, OUP Oxford, 1986.

Strandberg Publishing A/S
Gammel Mønt 14
DK-1117 Copenhagen
Denmark
www.strandbergpublishing.dk

The Danish edition of this book was published with the generous support of:

Arne V. Schleschs Fond